Hopi Quilting

Stitched Traditions
from an Ancient Community

Best Wishes
Carolyn O'Bagy Davis

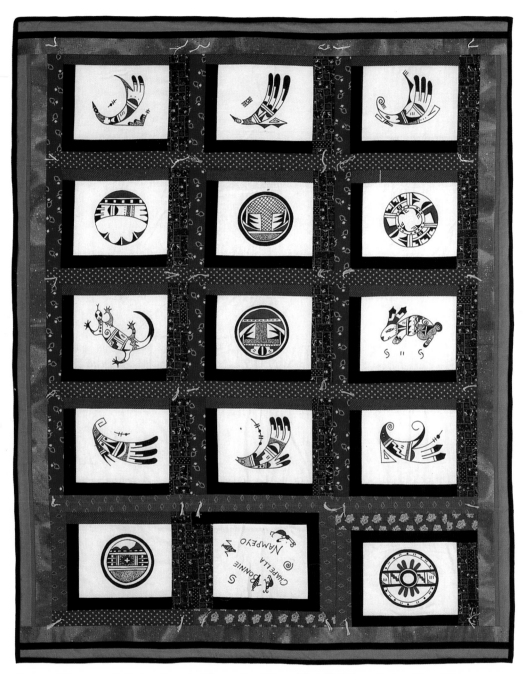

Painted Pottery Quilt by Bonnie Chapella, 62" x 49", 1996. Bonnie is a First Mesa potter and quilter who paints her quilt blocks with traditional Hopi pottery designs. She is a great-great granddaughter of the famous potter Nampeyo. Bonnie is also a fifth-generation quiltmaker. Black, browns, and other earth tones are her favorite colors to work with both in her quilts as well as in her ceramic art. Photography by David Elliott.

Hopi Quilting

Stitched Traditions from an Ancient Community

By Carolyn O'Bagy Davis

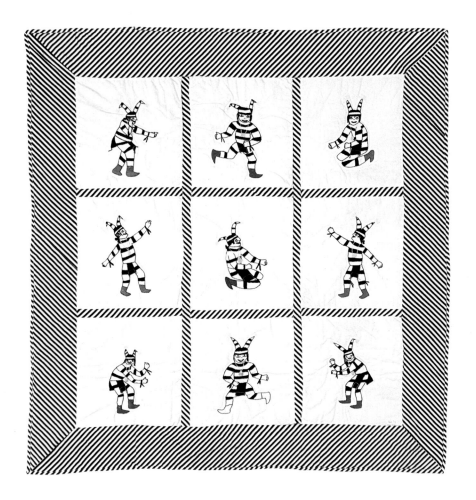

SANPETE PUBLICATIONS

Tucson, Arizona

Hopi woman at Bacavi showing a quilt top she pieced in Maria Schirmer's sewing class, 1940. Photograph courtesy of Mary Martha Baumgartner.

For Barbara O'Bagy, Cynthia Cobb, and Carole Collins with gratitude, and also with many thanks to the Hopi quilters who shared their stories and wonderful quilts.

Printed in the United States of America.

Book layout and design by Ken Graun.

Printed by Arizona Lithographers, Tucson, Arizona.

First Printing 1997.

ISBN: 0-9635092-3-3

Sanpete Publications • Post Office Box 85216 • Tucson, Arizona 85754-5216

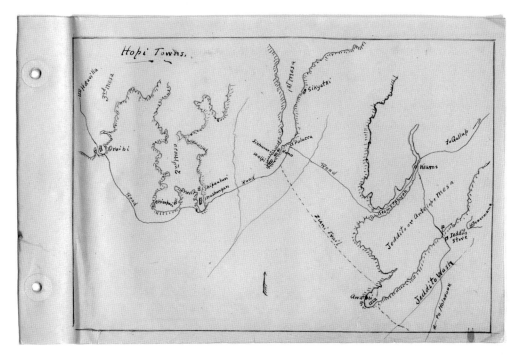

Hand-drawn map of the Hopi mesas by Hattie S. Cosgrove, 1923. First Mesa is located near the center of the map, with Second and Third Mesa to the west. Courtesy of C. Burton Cosgrove.

Contents

Joanna Quotskuyva's grandson, Christopher Noonkester, with a painted, Hopi boy quilt, 1997.

Marlene Sekaquaptewa's granddaughter, Linda Kewanimptewa, with one of the quilts she was given in a naming ceremony, 1995.

Author's Notes
and Acknowledgments

When we first began working on plans for a Museum of Northern Arizona Hopi quilt show—*Quilting from the Hopi Mesas: Stitched Traditions from an Ancient Community*—most people were astounded to learn that Hopis are quilters. Although explorers, tourists, anthropologists, missionaries, artists, and government workers have studied, photographed, and written about the Hopi people for well over a century, few had ever mentioned Hopi quiltmaking. The next predictable assumption seemed to be that if Hopis are quilters, then it was probably just a craft that a few of the women have recently learned.

Of course, that is a completely false notion. Hopi women have been quilting for well over a century, having learned the art from their mothers and grandmothers. And it is not an interest among just a few Hopis; rather, it is a common activity in every village on each of the three mesas. More than 135 quilters attended quilting workshops and planning sessions for the quilt show. And each trip to Hopi brought out additional women and several men who were interested in the quilt project.

It is quite remarkable that most people have overlooked Hopi quilts for such a long time. Most Hopi scholars expressed disbelief when asked about Hopi quilting. That Hopi quilts are somewhat "invisible" is all the more surprising when one considers that the arts and crafts of the Hopi people are much appreciated by the public, and are widely collected and studied by scholars, museums, and collectors.

It seems hard to believe that no one had ever noticed Hopi quilts. But when one starts to look, they are everywhere on the Hopi mesas: hanging on clotheslines, covering an oven door, draped on a bench, and covering many beds in Hopi homes. But their most common use seems to be as baby blankets. There are many beautiful babies and children on the Hopi mesas, and nearly every baby is wrapped in a handmade quilt.

I have been a quilter for most of my adult life—a fourth-generation quilter—and because of that interest I began to write the stories of pioneer women who made quilts. Naturally, I was curious about all of the Hopi quilts that I was seeing in the Hopi villages, and I began to chat with people about the quilts. I soon realized that every Hopi woman I talked with had a mother, grandmother, or aunt who made quilts. As I began to meet the quilters, our shared love of the art gave us much to discuss: favorite patterns and fabrics, the newest quilting techniques, rotary cutters and strip-piecing, and on and on. I became known as "the white woman who quilts." (Hopi people often refer to Anglos as "white people," such as when someone has a white teacher or a white friend. The Hopi word for Anglo is *Bahana*, sometimes *Pahaana*.)

Quilting gave us a common ground, but it also has the quality of not being a sacred tradition. The Hopi are a very private people, but the subject of quilting was not too sensitive, not too intrusive. Quilters everywhere love to talk of and share their work, and when we talked about quilting, none of the Hopi quilters was concerned about divulging too much of her culture. Quilts, even though they are used in some ceremonies and often hold deeply personal meaning, are tangible expressions of love and comfort. Even though some people think of it as just a "women's activity," quilting is a very important part of the daily work of many Hopi women, and through quilting one can begin to gain an insight into Hopi life.

The Museum of Northern Arizona invited Marlene Sekaquaptewa and me to curate an exhibit of Hopi quilts, and in the beginning it seemed that it would be a simple event. But as more people heard about the plans, the project grew and became more complicated. Quilters around the state of Arizona and beyond offered help and support. A Lila Wallace-Reader's Digest grant generously funded the major expenses for the exhibit, but there were many unforeseen expenses, and we had to search for additional funding. The Tucson Quilters Guild donated funds to purchase quilts for the exhibit, and several other guilds also gave

Walpi village on First Mesa, 1928. The steps to the left lead to the valley floor several hundred feet below Walpi. The path to the right leads to Sichomovi, the middle village on First Mesa. Photograph courtesy of Eleanor Means Hull.

donations for the show. It also was hoped that the exhibit would create a new market in selling quilts for the Hopi women, and a much needed source of income in the future.

The Hopi quilters were very excited about the show, but many of them expressed a desire to create a special quilt to enter in the exhibit. This was a concern because many quilters were stitching their quilts from fabric scraps, discarded clothing, and flour sacks. For many of them, lacking transportation to town and the money to purchase fine, new cottons for their quilts, that special quilt that they wanted to create for the exhibit was beyond reach.

Fortunately, quilters are a generous community. Members of the Tucson Quilters Guild and the Arizona Quilters Guild donated thousands of yards of fabric, hundreds of books, sewing machines, and boxes of quilting supplies to the Hopi quilters. V. I. P. Fabrics and South Sea Imports donated abundant quantities of fabric. Peggy Peck of the Quilt Basket in Tucson and Phyllis Sirrine of the Quilters Desert Patch in Sahuarita also gave yards of fabric, and Linda Britt sent boxes of designer fabrics. Laurene Sinema of the Quilted Apple in Phoenix donated funds to purchase quilts, and many sewing supplies. Gingher, Inc., gave us scissors, Mountain Mist donated 150 yards of quilt batting, Coats and Clark sent a case of sewing and quilting threads, and That Patchwork Place and ASN Publications contributed boxes of quilting books. In Tucson, Bruce and Mary Sue Lee of the Bernina Sewing Center and Mark Mayo of Ely's Vacuum and Sewing Center serviced and reconditioned almost a dozen donated sewing machines.

Quilting teachers Penny Burroughs, Janet Carruth, Carole Collins, and Barbara O'Bagy volunteered their time to travel to Hopi to teach free workshops in each village (of course, the Hopi quilters were all interested in learning some of the newest quilting patterns and techniques). Dee Lynn and Audrey Waite sponsored a Hopi quilter to attend Quilt Camp in the Pines. Cynthia Cobb helped with donations and organizing. As we traveled to each mesa to conduct the quilt workshops, the number of interested Hopi quilters grew to more than 135. In an effort to speed communications with all of the quilters, several Hopi women volunteered to be local coordinators. I wish to extend a great thanks to Lillian Tallas of Moencopi, Bernita Mahkewa and Eileen Randolph of Bacavi, Janice Dennis of Kykotsmovi, and Karen Tootsie of Keams Canyon. They helped organize the quilting workshops, shared information, and gave valuable input on the exhibit.

A Friendship Quilt was planned early in the project. Hopi women and Anglo quilters across the Southwest were invited to decorate a quilt block with their name, clan, town or village, quilt guild logo, and any other decoration they wished to add. Carole Collins designed and assembled the top and hand quilted the quilt which was donated to the permanent collection of the Museum of Northern Arizona. The Friendship Quilt embodies the spirit of friendship and cooperation between Hopi and other Southwestern quilters.

As we realized we would need more funding for many of the activities that we hoped to plan while the exhibit was hung, we naturally, as quilters, turned to quilt-related events to make those plans a reality. A small quilt auction was planned for which quilts were solicited from quilters around the country. Several guilds even organized Hopi committees to stitch small quilts. Audrey Waite of Sedona, Arizona, offered to chair and coordinate plans for the event, and Ed Devlin of Taos, New Mexico, donated his services to travel to Flagstaff to serve as auctioneer.

Rita Nuvangyaoma, Shipaulovi.

Others who have contributed to the project are Heather Boushley, C. Burton Cosgrove, Allen Dart, Helen Young Frost, Peggy Hazard, Michaella Keener, Alexander Lindsay, Andreas Punzel, Emory Sekaquaptewa, David Shaul, Helga Teiwes, Peter Whiteley, John Thiessen of Bethel College, North Newton, Kansas, Susan Willett, and Kathy Hubenschmidt and Susan Luebberman of the Arizona State Museum, University of Arizona. Eleanor Means Hull loaned her mother's photographs and diaries, and Mary Martha Baumgartner also shared her mother's stories and photographs. Laurie Webster was a source of vital information that she always generously shared.

Friendship Quilt, pieced and quilted by Carole Collins. Blocks were signed and decorated by Anglo and Hopi quilters throughout Arizona. Many of the Anglo quilters decorated their blocks with their quilt guild logos. Hopi quilters used their clan signs. Photography by David Elliott.

Working among the Hopi quilters has been a life-changing experience. It has been an honor to be invited into people's homes and to form valued friendships with many of the Hopi ladies. In many ways, visiting the Hopi mesas is much like stepping back in time. There may be a satellite dish on the roof, but many of the old stone homes are otherwise timeless. Some of the quilters live in houses that they inherited from their mothers and grandmothers in an unbroken line that goes many hundreds of years back into the past.

Florence Crannell Means, author of *Sunlight on the Hopi Mesas*, visited her friend Abigail Johnson in February 1928. Abigail was a Baptist missionary at Second Mesa. Florence wrote in her journal that she arrived in Winslow, Arizona, during a snowstorm. The 75-mile-trip up to the mesa took more than four hours to drive "over the snowy desert." Every morning at the mission home they awoke to "ice in the wash-bowl." The same trip today is accomplished in about an hour, and there was never an ice-filled washbowl in the morning, but there was always a deep awareness of a timeless community in a starkly beautiful landscape.

Carole Collins, one of the volunteer quilting teachers who went to Hopi several times, was also deeply affected. She wrote, "My favorite 'treasures' from Hopi are two patchwork potholders I bought from Pearl Nuvangyaoma for twenty-five cents each. I use them every day, and I hear her. We said twenty-five cents was too little to sell them for—and she said, 'I don't charge much. I want my friends to be able to have my things.' Well, I don't presume friendship, but I do certainly have her 'things'—Pearl's living room with the boxes and bags of tops and aprons and quilts and stuff—all over the floor—and us there in the middle of it. And all those photographs of family members that covered the walls. And Pearl sitting there dignified and secure. I really got my quarter's worth."

Truly, the trips to the Hopi mesas and the visits with so many of the Hopi quilters have been memorable, treasured experiences.

Many companies and individuals have contributed to this project, and whether we live in the deserts of southern Arizona or up on the Hopi mesas, we have all benefited immensely from this great sharing of quilting. A last expression of great thanks must be extended to Dr. Edwin Wade and the staff at the Museum of Northern Arizona who offered so much support and encouragement. Through their efforts, Hopi quilters are able to share with the public their remarkable quilts that are a unique blending of traditional quilting and Hopi imagery.

Hopi blanket weaver, 1914. Photograph by Karl Moon. Courtesy of the Museum of Northern Arizona.

Foreword

Chance acquaintances are typically fleeting, yet occasionally an instant rapport emerges into a productive friendship. Such was the outcome of my meeting with Carolyn Davis in the parking lot of the Museum of Northern Arizona. The topic of our first impromptu chat was archaeology and the ancient Mimbres people of southern New Mexico, but somehow the conversation meandered northward, eventually reaching the weathered Hopi mesas of northeastern Arizona. The talk revolved around pots, Indian art shops, and local crafts, and then Carolyn mentioned Hopi quilts. She gently traversed the 120-year cultural landscape of quilting in Hopiland, from its introduction by Anglos to what has now become a profoundly Hopi tradition. Though I had known Hopi intimately for over thirty years, somehow all this had missed me. As is true of many anthropologists, I had been concerned with the "big stuff," like political structures, linguistics, and belief systems. In exploring these areas with primarily male involvement, I had been excluded from, or had excluded myself from, an entire universe created by female quilters. Quilts, these creations of the heart that enrich a world through skill of hand and passion of devotion had eluded me. Suddenly, for me, Hopi took on a new complexion; it was filled with a population of vibrant women, both young and old, creating a unique art solely for its own sake. The deeply personal art of the quilt reverberated with the spirit of its makers. The hopes, memories, successes, and failures of individual lives condensed over the generation into the weave of a larger fabric which bespoke a people's history. And in this history the gift of voice was handed down, decade upon decade, from mother to daughter, from village to city, and now from the Old World to the new. Here was a story waiting to be heard, an exhibition and a book to exalt the creative potential of the human spirit.

In a museum's parking lot we pledged our energies to these ends. A year later, a bit chastened and more subdued by the realities of the undertaking, we celebrate through this book and the exhibition it accompanies, the fortitude and creativity of Hopi quilters, of Hopi women—and in particular, of 136 Hopi women whose enthusiastic involvement has made this book and exhibition possible. It is their story.

Through the gift of the quilt a bridge has been built across language and cultural barriers. Across this bridge have poured gifts going both directions. The Tucson Quilters' Guild has sent materials, resources, and technical support to the Mesas, and Hopi women have shared their skills with Anglo quilters in workshops on Second and Third Mesas. Hopi women have accepted scholarships to university workshops at Northern Arizona University and elsewhere. The magazine *Arizona Highways* presents Hopi quilting in a feature-length story and a PBS special filmed under the inspired direction of Pam Stevenson brings the Hopi quilting tradition to a national audience. Through quilts Hopi and western women now meet in the cooperative spirit of shared creativity, and in the age-old enclave of the sewing bee build understanding among one another.

Through quilts this shared passion now enriches two worlds and contributes beauty unselfishly to the unfolding future of both. Through quilts, a random conversation grew into a circle of friendship embracing Carolyn Davis, Pam Stevenson, Museum of Northern Arizona staff members Deb Hill, David Wilcox, Mike Fox, Pat Neary, Kate Sibley, and—to my great good fortune—myself. Congratulations to Carolyn Davis on the fruition of her vision and labor fully and lastingly visible in this publication.

Edwin L. Wade
Deputy Director, Museum of Northern Arizona

Heart Quilt, by Maude Nasetoynewa, 49" x 49", 1977. Maude Nasetoynewa is a Moencopi quilter. She appliquéd blue hearts onto peach-colored blocks with a blanket stitch.

Introduction

by Marlene Sekaquaptewa

The first contact I had with Carolyn Davis was a telephone call she made to me after reading *Me and Mine*, the story of Helen Sekaquaptewa, my mother. Since that conversation many other talks have taken place, as well as a Hopi quilt exhibit and the emergence of a Hopi quilting network in our villages. Carolyn Davis has skillfully complied this volume for the exhibit with a wonderful sense of insight, compassion, and understanding. Many Hopi women shared treasured quilting memories and experiences.

One of my first memories was watching my mother quilt. I was fascinated with how she put those pretty pieces of cloth together, and I wanted to know how she did it. During the long, dark winter evenings my mother would cut up old clothes into quilt blocks. I remember one evening when my brother wanted her attention, but she was so engrossed in her sewing. Finally he asked Mother, "Why do you have to do that?" And my mother quietly replied that everyone needed a quilt. Quilting was always a part of her life, and she passed that love on to me. As soon as I could handle a needle and thread, my mother made sure I mastered the skills "of domestic arts."

I always knew that quilting had been here for a long time. My mother talked about tourists, doctors, and missionaries. That's where I first heard about sewing. My mother said the missionaries didn't just teach us about god and religion, they also brought us farm implements and other goods, and of course, cloth. Then later the traders brought fabric. It was calico. The ladies loved this new cloth, it was soft, bright, lightweight—you could do so much with it.

At school my mother loved the white man's clothing. It was not as scratchy as the traditional Hopi dress made of wool. She was given three uniforms, two for every day and one special dress for Sunday. When she came home, my mother would wear a cotton dress under her *manta*— with the sleeves rolled up so that her mother would not know she was wearing that clothing under her traditional dress. Her mother did not approve, and she scolded my mother whenever she caught her wearing those clothes.

Eventually the women got cloth at the trading posts, and they made simple, gathered dresses of calico. And once the ladies saw quilting at the church they always went back. At school all of the girls learned to sew. The older girls made clothes and uniforms for the younger children. In the villages sewing was always a topic of conversation. When someone was ill, all of the women would donate blocks to her if all she could do was sit and piece quilt tops. In hospitals the missionaries would take blocks for the ill person to sew to pass the hours.

In the 1960s and 1970s there was a great revival of quilting around the country, and we were all excited about the new books and fabrics. Since the early years, quilting has become a part of daily life here. It is a routine activity, as well as being useful and a favorite pastime. More important, with our extended families and clan associations, quilts have become a vital link to the special ties in family relationships. The women of my generation have inherited the interest and skills of quilting through our mothers and grandmothers as illustrated by the wonderful stories in the following pages.

 Marlene Sekaquaptewa

Hopi potter, Hano Pueblo, Hopi, Arizona, c. 1911. This unidentified First Mesa woman is painting a pottery bowl. In traditional Hopi homes, quilts and blankets were stored away during the daytime by folding them and hanging them from a lodge pole, or *tuulata*, hung from the ceiling. Photo by H. F. Robinson. Negative No. 37030. Courtesy of the Museum of New Mexico.

Quilting bee at Third Mesa, conducted by Mennonite missionary Maria Schirmer, c. 1940s. Photograph courtesy of Mary Martha Baumgartner.

Hopi Quilting

Stitched Traditions from an Ancient Community

Hopi women—and some men—have been quilting since the 1880s. Quilting is a craft that was introduced to the Hopi mesas by missionaries and teachers, and over the decades the practice of quiltmaking has taken a secure place in the hearts and culture of the Hopi people. In earlier times, coverings for warmth were woven by Hopi men from cotton that was grown in their fields, or wool from sheep brought into the Southwest in the sixteenth century by Spanish explorers. Warm coverings were also made by Hopi women who wove strips of rabbit hides into soft fur blankets.

By the late nineteenth century, with the increasing availability of affordable, factory-produced fabrics that could be purchased in the trading posts, and the free quilt patches from the missionaries, quilting became a widely practiced activity on the Hopi mesas. Hopi women today are third- and fourth-generation quilters with a strong patchwork tradition and a firmly established love of the craft. Quilting bees are a weekly activity among the women at the mission churches and village community centers.

Over the decades, the use of quilts, *tavupu*, has spread into many areas of Hopi life, far beyond their original intended purpose as bed

Bear's Paw Quilt by Lucille Namoki, 38" x 51", 1997. Lucille Namoki is a potter and quilter from Kykotsmovi. She hand pieced and tied her Bear's Paw Quilt. Photography by David Elliott.

covers. Quilts are now used in some important Hopi rituals, most notably the Baby Naming Ceremony, *tipos'asni*. And at the end of life, when there is a death, a quilt is often used as a burial shroud. As in the wider quilting community, quilts are used as gifts of love and caring. They are often given at weddings, graduations, or other special times in a person's life. When a son or daughter leaves their village to go away to school, to work, or for military service, a quilt is often sent along as a warm remembrance of home and family.

As a rule, Hopi quilters do not make presentation quilts: quilts that are meant only to be looked at, not used, quilts to be passed down through the generations as family heirlooms. Hopi quilts may be gifts of love and caring, but they also are practical items, and they are meant to be used. Economics dictate that Hopi quilts are made of fabric scraps, used clothing, and unmatched quilt blocks sent to mission churches. Unlike urban quilters who have greater access to the newest supplies and often purchase yards of color-coordinated cotton fabric for their quilts, Hopi quilters stitch their tops from a varied array of fabrics, colors, and patterns, creating quilts that have a spontaneous and exciting feeling. Their graphics are often stunning. They are all a pleasure to behold.

Color and movement are essential components of Hopi quilts. The late Florence Pulford, who was a scholar of the Morning Star Quilts of the

Bacavi quilters showing a Trip Around the World Quilt, c. 1950s. Photograph courtesy of the Mennonite Library and Archives, Bethel College, North Newton, Kansas.

northern Plains Indian women, said, "Color is the essence of Indian quilting" (Pulford 1989: 8). The introduction of quilting in the 1880s, along with the bright colors of gaily printed calicos, was an exciting new art form to Native American women. Even though they often had only flour sacks and used clothing available for their sewing, the combination of the new fabrics with piecing quilt tops opened great new vistas of creativity.

Many Hopi quilters love bright fabrics, perhaps as a response to their landscape where the sand and stone, with only sparse vegetation, tends to be a tan monotone. Red is a favorite choice to be incorporated into a quilt, and bright yellows, blues, and greens are also often chosen. Movement and graphics are also a strong part of Hopi quilts. The quilters easily overcome the shortcomings of scrapbags filled with unmatched colors, patterns, and textures to stitch inspiring works of fabric art.

Hopi quilters make their quilts to be given freely and easily as gifts. Sometimes they are stitched together on short notice if an event arises where a quilt is needed. Perfection is not always the goal; the gift of a quilt is the higher aim. It is almost unthinkable that a quilt would be made as a showpiece, only to be brought out on a special occasion, and never to be used as a wrap or bed covering. Hopi quilts are made to be used, loved, and in the process, worn out. Even quilts made by long-gone

Fields at Moencopi, c. 1920s. Photograph courtesy of Mary May Bailey.

mothers and grandmothers are not treasured and hoarded away. They are given to grandchildren, nieces, and nephews. They are used in everyday life, and the recipients know they are using a quilt stitched by someone who loved them. For this reason, and also because of the extensive use of quilts for burials, almost no old Hopi quilts exist.

There are, however, wonderful stories of old-time quilting among the Hopis. Vintage photos show glimpses of quilts being used to wrap babies, to carry a load of corn, or as a ground covering to sit upon, but the only old quilts still in existence are a few that were carried away by missionaries and traders, and some that were overlooked in trunks and boxes. Just a very few of these older quilts have fortunately been preserved, and they are quite rare. The Hopi quilting tradition comes from an older time when quilts were made of scraps, made out of necessity. They still are a practical item, stitched for warmth and given with love.

The Hopi People

The Hopi people have lived on Black Mesa in the *Hopi Tutskwa* (Hopi Lands) in the northeastern part of Arizona for a millenium. Their ancestors are thought to be the *Hisatsinom*, the ancient cliff-dwelling people who have lived in northern Arizona and the Four Corners region since the prehistoric Basket Maker times. The Hopi village of Oraibi on Third Mesa is considered to be the oldest continuously inhabited community in North America. Using pottery and tree-ring dates from roof beams, archaeologists have determined that the village's origins date back to A. D. 1150. Other Hopi villages are at least 300 years old.

Black Mesa is a high plateau in northeastern Arizona. Three finger-like extensions form the mesas where the Hopi people built their villages so many centuries ago. At present, there are thirteen villages on First, Second, and Third Mesa and to the west along Moencopi Wash. There are approximately eleven thousand Hopis today, but in spite of these numbers, their ancient homelands are now completely surrounded by the larger Navajo Nation.

The traditional Hopi homes are small and simple, constructed of rock with adobe-mud mortar, and built apartment-style in several terraced levels with contiguous rooms. In each village there are plazas, open areas for dances and social events, and underground kivas where many ceremonial activities take place. Shrines are located in the plazas and also near the villages. These are sacred places where offerings, prayers, and thanks are given.

Life is hard and spare in this arid and wind-swept land. Little rain falls and temperatures range from blistering summers to bitterly cold winters. In 1875, W. B. Truax, United States Indian Agent to the Hopi Pueblos, wrote in his annual report to the Commissioner of Indian Affairs that the Hopi mesas are

> a very unpromising place for any human beings to attempt to make a subsistence either by cultivating the soil or raising stock. And yet the Indians are so strongly attached to this poor and forbidding place that they cannot be induced to entertain any proposition for their changing to a better one. Probably there is no tribe more devotedly attached to the homes and graves of their fathers than the Moquis [Hopi] Pueblos [Truax 1875: 211].

Hopi beanfield south of Hotevilla, 1923. Courtesy of C. Burton Cosgrove.

Crazy Quilt top by Grace Masawistewa, 86" x 63", c. 1950s. Grace machine pieced this quilt top by stitching scraps of silk and satin onto squares of muslin and flour sacking. Some of the colorful fabrics in this top came from vintage ties. Grace enjoyed doing embroidery, and some of the blocks show her decorative feather stitching. Perhaps she eventually planned to embroider around each piece in the Crazy Quilt. Grace's daughter, Janice Dennis, recalled that her mother often finished the edges of her quilts by hand sewing with an overcast stitch. Quilt courtesy of Janice Dennis. Photography by David Elliott.

Agriculture is crucial for the tribal existence. Men farm small fields in the flat country below the mesas, growing corn, beans, squash, melons, and cotton. Corn is the most important crop, both for its importance as a food and for its spiritual significance. Several types of corn are cultivated, including sweet corn, field corn, blue corn, and red, yellow, and white corn. Some of these varieties are native strains adapted by the Hopis over the many centuries that they have been farming in the Four Corners country.

Because the farming plots can be some distance from the mesa top villages, Hopi men traditionally ran great distances each day down to the valley floor farms to tend their crops, and then back up to the villages at the end of the day. In earlier times, before there was a Hopi settlement at Moencopi, the men from Third Mesa generally ran forty miles to tend their fields, and the next day ran all the way back to their village homes. In addition to the farming plots there are almost hidden, terraced gardens that drape downward along the protected edges of the mesa canyons. Nurtured by springs, the tiny family plots produce lush varieties of herbs and kitchen vegetables. The terraced garden sections are passed down from family to family within clan affiliations, as are the larger valley farmlands.

Little rain and poor soils make existence difficult, but a rich cycle of religious ceremonials offers an incredible balance to the harsh mesa life for the Hopi people. Bringing rain is a focus of Hopi spiritual life. Highly perfected farming skills produce crops in an area where any other people would doubt that a blade of grass could be coaxed to grow. Most people who know the Hopi to any degree are sympathetic to their belief that the religious ceremonies of the Hopi priests do bring the rains. Over the centuries, the land and the sun and the annual ceremonial cycles have become tightly interwoven (Whiteley 1988: 73).

The Hopis believe that their people came into this world from an opening in the ground near the Grand Canyon, at the bottom of the Little Colorado Canyon and just above its juncture with the Colorado River. This holy place of emergence is the *sipapu*, and the world that we live in today is the Fourth World. When a person dies, his spirit becomes a kachina, or *katsina*, who dwells for part of the year in the world of the dead, the underworld, and for part of the year in the Hopi mesas where kachinas perform ceremonies to bring crops and rain.

The Hopis have long been known for their remarkable ceremonies and dances. Through the calendar year, each changing season brings an elaborate array of dances and rituals. In December the kachinas return to the villages. Masked dancers represent the arrival of the kachina spirits in the Hopi towns. Through the spring and early summer, dances and ceremonies are held to bring rain and make the crops grow. When a Hopi man performs in a kachina ceremony he becomes one with the spirit of the kachina. If he dances with a good heart his efforts will indeed bring the clouds and the rain so necessary for crops and survival. In July, the

Traditional handwoven, striped blankets hang in front of a house in Shipaulovi, 1923. Courtesy of C. Burton Cosgrove.

Traditional storage room in a Hopi house, c. 1912–1922. Great quantities of corn are stored away, and blankets and quilts are folded and stacked in a corner. The sacks that held grains and flour were later used for piecing quilts. Courtesy of the Kopta Collection, Museum of Northern Arizona.

Second Mesa, 1923. The two villages of Mishongnovi and Shipaulovi are barely visible on top of the rocky mesa. Courtesy of C. Burton Cosgrove.

Niman, or Home Dance, is performed when the kachinas go back to their homes in the San Francisco Peaks, the beautiful snow capped mountains southwest of the Hopi country.

Hopi society is matrilineal. Membership in a clan is inherited through a child's mother, and relationships are traced through the mother's side of the family. Women own the houses and ownership is passed from mother to daughter. After marriage, the groom moves in with his wife's family. Through clan affiliation each Hopi individual enjoys a vast, extended family. Although homes are passed from mother to daughter, farming land is communally owned by clans or related families of the same clan.

Women have many responsibilities, caring for the children and providing a good home for their families. Traditionally, First Mesa women made pottery, while women from Second and Third Mesa wove baskets and plaques. Food preparation is a never ending task for Hopi women. Corn is the staple food, indeed, corn literally is life to the Hopis. More than just an important food crop, corn holds deeply significant and symbolic meaning in Hopi life.

From the time the ears of corn are carried in from the fields, it is the woman's job to dry the corn, shell it, and eventually grind hundreds of pounds of cornmeal for the many dishes and drinks that are prepared with corn. Many of the foods made with corn are not simply traditional recipes, they are dishes interwoven with religious ceremonies, and their preparation and consumption have important spiritual symbolism.

In earlier times corn was ground by hand on a stone, a metate. Today, however, women use electric mills or simply purchase cornmeal at a store. Generally, the only corn that is still hand ground is the white corn that is used for ceremonial purposes. Even though the bulk of a family's corn is electrically ground, and some of it is purchased in stores, the traditional activities of growing corn, holding ceremonies to bring the rain,

Adrienne Stray Calf, 1997, Second Mesa. Adrienne's grandfather taught her to knit the traditional Hopi leggings. He instructed her to knit in a spiral, and he said that it was just like life, "Life goes round and round and no matter how tired you get you have got to keep going until you finish it." Her grandfather's knitting needles were handmade from wooden dowels. He used five needles and they were polished with linseed oil.

and the long and intricate preparation of special corn-based dishes are still tightly integrated into daily Hopi life.

Hopi men are farmers, growing food for their families and cotton for blankets and clothing. Traditionally, Hopi men spun, wove, and stitched the fabric for clothes and ceremonial garments. When the Spanish priests and explorers brought sheep to the Southwest in the sixteenth century, wool replaced some of the cotton textiles used by the Hopis. In early times the Hopis were known as the growers and suppliers of cotton to the people in the Four Corners region. An archaeologist referred to cotton as one of the most precious assets in the prehistoric Southwest because "in societies without rare metals, fibers woven into cloth are often extremely valuable." In addition to the use of cotton for clothing and blankets, it was used to make "the ceremonial kilts, sashes, burial shrouds, and symbolic string used in pueblo rituals" (Walker 1996: 4).

Southwestern scholar Kate Peck Kent noted that the Hopi were "functioning as a major center for production and distribution of fiber and cloth" at least from the early sixteenth century (Kent 1983: 29). Kent also asserted that cotton held an extremely high value as a trade item. Furthermore, by the fourteenth century, cotton had become "symbolically associated with clouds in rain magic," which greatly enhanced its practical as well as spiritual significance.

Through the long winters, Hopi men gathered in the kivas where they spun and wove wool and cotton fibers into lengths of fabric. In their

Hopi man knitting leggings, 1898. Negative No. 1082. Courtesy of the California Historical Society, Title Insurance and Trust Photo Collection, Department of Special Collections, University of Southern California Library.

homes, they also wove and stitched everyday clothing and blankets for their families. A woman's dress, a *manta*, was a simple, straight tube-shaped garment, calf-length, that secured over one shoulder, leaving the other one bare. Blankets were woven with broad black and white stripes or plaid patterns.

Ceremonial garments such as dance kilts and wedding clothes are still made in the kivas, but today Hopi people purchase western dress for everyday wear. Traditional garments are only worn for special ceremonial or public events. Nowadays, many ceremonial garments are woven by the men and then decorated with designs stitched with colored

A Hopi man brings a flock of sheep back to the stone corral below the mesa rim, 1928. Photograph courtesy of Eleanor Means Hull.

threads or woolen yarns. Men also knit black or white leggings that are used for sacred dances and ceremonies.

During prehistoric times leggings were made with a looping technique, but it is likely that knitting was introduced to the Hopis, along with sheep and wool products, by the Spanish. Archaeologists discovered two knitted fragments from the excavations of the abandoned Hopi settlement of Awatovi. These knitted fragments date from the second half of the seventeenth century. Leggings and woven blankets were two items that the Spanish government demanded as tribute from the pueblo peoples. In the Eastern Pueblos of New Mexico women knitted most of the tribute items, but there are early accounts of Zuni and Hopi men knitting (interview with Laurie Webster, 1997).

Because the men were the primary textile workers among the Hopis, they seem to have been the ones who learned to knit. Vintage photographs show Hopi men and boys knitting, and many of the contemporary Hopi quilters recall that their fathers and grandfathers were knitters. Leggings were knit in a spiral using five knitting needles made from straight, thin sticks with points carved on each end. Some men knit colored bands into their leggings, while others used decorative patterns with cables, popcorn stitches, and zigzags. One woman recalled that her

A Hopi man, Kutka, spinning wool or cotton thread, c. 1905–1912. The threads would later be woven into sashes, blankets, and garments. Courtesy of the Kate Cory Collection, Museum of Northern Arizona.

grandfather could knit without looking at his work. In fact, he generally watched television while he was knitting.

Another important covering that was made for warmth was the rabbit blanket that Hopi women wove from strips of rabbit pelts. Thin strips of skins with the fur still intact were soaked in water to soften them. Next they were wrapped around yucca or wool fibers. As the strips dried they tightened into a fluffy cord. This cordage was then woven into a soft blanket (Kent 1983: 25). These fur blankets, sometimes called rabbit quilts today, were made by the Hopis for hundreds of years. Remnants of these blankets have been found in ancient sites and were still being woven by Hopi women in the early years of the twentieth century.

From outward appearances it may seem that the Hopis have become westernized. Through the last four centuries, outside groups have

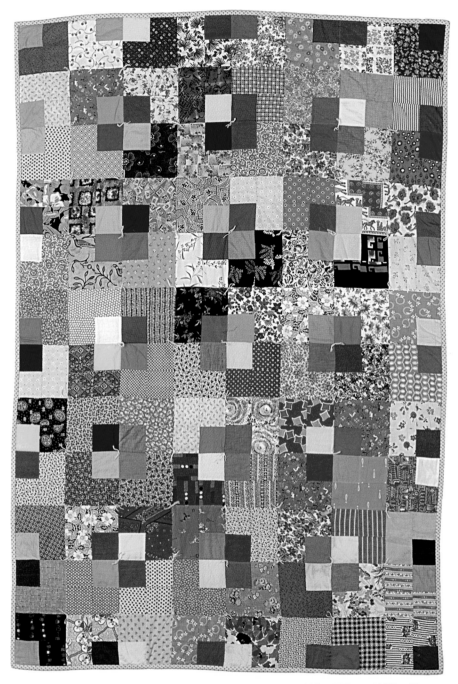

Four Patch Variation Quilt by Grace Masawistewa, 83" x 55", c. 1950s. Grace Masawistewa was a prolific quiltmaker. When she passed away in 1995, she left fifteen unfinished quilt tops. Her daughter, Janice Dennis, inherited several of the tops and plans to finish them. This quilt was one of the tops that was recently finished.

The Four Patch Variation Quilt is hand pieced. Many of the print fabrics are flour sacking. The imaginative use of print and solid fabric in each block gives this appealing scrap quilt an interesting geometric effect. Quilt courtesy of Janice Dennis. Photography by David Elliott.

exerted much pressure to change the Hopi way of life. But in spite of some changes, the Hopi people have retained their culture and religion to a degree that is not found in many other Native American peoples. They are a deeply religious people, and they still widely practice their traditional rituals in an intricate year-long ceremonial cycle.

Life is hard for the Hopis, in spite of their adaptation of many modern innovations. Their land is poor and barren, and they live far from urban centers and the schools, stores, hospitals, and conveniences that most people take for granted today. But in a striking contrast to their external environment, is a rich religious and ceremonial heritage, and a close and extensive family network. These qualities make Hopi life vibrant and full. Judy Tuwaletstiwa is an artist and poet who lives at Kykotsmovi near Third Mesa. She concisely described her environment when she stated, "Life at Hopi is hard, but it is beautiful."

Quilting Comes to the Hopi Mesas

The Hopi are a peaceful, agricultural people, but over the ages they have withstood the attacks and pressures from their neighbors and outside groups. In early times they were victims of raids from the Utes and Navajos. The arrival of the Spanish priests and explorers in A. D. 1540 brought strong influences to renounce traditional beliefs and convert to Christianity. There often were severe consequences and punishments for those who resisted.

The second half of the nineteenth century brought *Pahaanas*, Anglos, who worked relentlessly over the next century to remake, educate, convert, and westernize the Hopis. Missionaries came early to the mesas. Jacob Hamblin led the first group of Mormon missionaries to Hopi country in 1858. In 1870 the United States government established an agency headquarters at Oraibi, and in the same year a Moravian mission church was also built at Oraibi. Four years later the agency was moved east to Keams Canyon. In 1893 Mennonite missionaries Heinrich and Martha Voth located their church at Oraibi.

Other denominations also sent their emissaries. The Baptists founded a mission at Mishongnovi on Second Mesa, and in 1894 established another mission at Polacca on First Mesa. Baptist missionary Abigail Johnson, who arrived at Polacca in 1901, spent most of her adult life working among the Hopis. Miss McLean, another early Baptist missionary, admired the Hopis in many ways, but felt it her Christian duty to remake them. In 1902 she wrote,

> The Hopis are a poor people, not only in things spiritual but in things temporal. How they manage to make a living is a wonder; white men would starve if they had to depend on the resources within reach of these Indians for subsistence. They are the most

The group of people in this vintage Hopi photo have most likely gathered to watch a dance or ceremony. The child in the left center of the photograph is dressed in a pieced, dress-like garment that appears to have been stitched together with decorative embroidery and feather stitching. Negative No. 41686. Courtesy of the Arizona Historical Society.

A quilt is thrown over a clothesline in this vintage photograph of a Hopi house. Courtesy of the Museum of Northern Arizona.

Hopi man stitching a garment, c. 1898–1901. Negative No. 3671. Courtesy of the California Historical Society, Title Insurance and Trust Photo Collection, Department of Special Collections, University of Southern California Library.

active Indians I have known. They don't mind running 30 miles a day, and are always wanting to work. Their country is a dreary, barren waste, and the people are pitiably superstitious and degraded [*Thirty-Six Years Among Indians 1914: 48*].

Miss Mary Kelley, who joined Miss McLean two years later, reported, "I feel more like a foreign missionary than a home missionary, for these people are as truly heathen as any can be across the waters, and it will take time, perseverance, prayer, and faith for their conversion" (*Thirty-Six Years Among Indians* 1914: 52). Miss Kelley did concede, however, that there were many things in their favor. She noted that the Hopis were industrious and peaceable and showed much affection for their children. They seemed contented, even though they were extremely poor. Their homes only had dirt floors, and there was little furniture. At night they "roll themselves up in sheepskin rugs and quilts and sleep on the floor."

Since the time of early contacts, the Hopi people have been subjected to intense missionary pressure. Much of the attention from Christian churches was a result of the peaceful, agricultural life that the Hopis follow. Their culture had many qualities that Anglos admired and emulated. With the end of the Indian wars of the nineteenth century, the American public and government officials felt that the path to solving "the Indian problem" was in westernizing—and converting—Native Americans. The ultimate goal was to obliterate their culture through blending Indian peoples with white society.

The Hopis were a sedentary, farming people, but their religion was far removed from Christianity. As a consequence, many denominations sent missionaries to convert the Hopis. Preachers held street meetings in the village plazas, and hymns played on portable organs attracted some Hopis to listen to the sermons. But the most reliable tool for drawing people to the churches was the weekly sewing and quilting bees. When missionaries realized that both Hopi men and women enjoyed the bees, they became a fixture on the Hopi mesas.

While the Christian missionaries tried to change the Hopis largely through friendly persuasion, Indian agents and school superintendents had the full power—and force—of the American government behind them. They exerted tremendous pressure upon the Hopi people to give up their ancient religion and culture. Christianity and western education were forced upon the Hopis.

At first, Hopi children were just expected to attend day schools. Teachers cut the children's hair and dressed them in western clothes. But many families could not be relied upon to send their children to school

A Hopi man at his sewing. Courtesy of the Museum of Northern Arizona.

Second Mesa Day School Quilt, 69" x 62", 1992. Alfreda Secakuku helped her second grade class decorate the blocks for this charming quilt in 1992. Each student painted a block with images that were meaningful to them and signed their name. Caradina drew her family and her house, Demetria painted a bowl of corn. This charming and colorful quilt also depicts kachinas, mudheads, a kiva, a pueblo, and two smiley faces. Ada Fredericks assembled the quilt top. Quilt courtesy of Alfreda Secakuku. Photography by David Elliott.

every day. One Indian agent noted that "to place these wild children under a teacher's care but four or five hours a day, and permit them to spend the other nineteen in the filth and degradation of the village, makes the attempt to educate and civilize them a mere farce" (Adams 1995: 29). When the Hopis refused to send their children to school, soldiers were brought in to round them up, often using rough and frightening tactics. These raids generally occurred at night or near dawn. Fathers who protested were arrested and sent away to prisons. Through all of these decades of persistent persuasion to change, to give up their old ways, the Hopi people have clung tenaciously to their traditions. They have, however, adopted some beneficial Western ideas.

Quiltmaking was one tradition that was freely accepted and integrated into Hopi life. Perhaps the degree to which Hopis accept quilting is not surprising given the long tradition of working with cotton, wool, and textiles, and the strong association of certain garments and textiles with important Hopi ceremonies. Across the continent women have commonly stitched quilts to mark significant life passages. Quilts have been made to celebrate births and marriages, to remember a friend, or to mourn a passing. Within this long-held tradition of piecing a quilt to honor the large and small events of life, Hopi quilters have blended quilting with their unique culture and lifestyles. Today the events and passages of life at Hopi are most commonly marked with the gift or creation of a quilt.

Students at the Phoenix Indian High School showing off their stitched handwork, c. 1950s. Courtesy of the Bureau of Indian Affairs Archives, Phoenix Area Office.

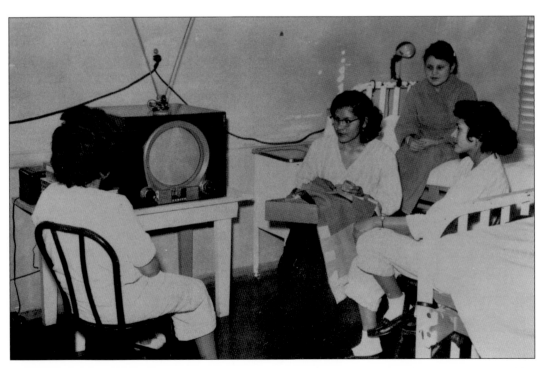

Students in the infirmary at the Phoenix Indian High School watching television, c. 1950s. The student seated in the center is piecing a quilt top. Courtesy of the Bureau of Indian Affairs Archives, Phoenix Area Office.

Government Schools

From the beginning, education has been both a blessing and a curse to the Hopis. In the early years many Hopis did not want their children to be sent to government schools. They, in fact, wanted nothing to do with the outsiders who came to their country and disrupted their lives and culture. There were bitter struggles with Indian agents, police, and soldiers who forced education upon the Hopis. At first, children were sent to the Keams Canyon School that was established in 1887. The school was built on land purchased from the trader Thomas Keam, who had opened his trading post in 1878. Even though the school was on Hopi land, it was a long wagon ride to the site on the far eastern edge of the reservation.

In later years children were taken away to the boarding school in Phoenix, Arizona, or sent to distant schools scattered around the country. For most families this meant long separations of months and even years, and this was difficult even for families who valued the benefits of

Students at the Phoenix Indian High School showing off their dresses stitched in sewing classes, c. 1950s. Two of the girls are wearing what was commonly known as "squaw dresses," a popular style with women across the country in the 1950s. The style is similar to the velvet skirts and blouses still worn by many Navajo women in Arizona and New Mexico, and they were a popular tourist item in the Southwest. Generally, the outfit was a skirt and blouse with gathers at the neckline and waist. The full skirt was often constructed with three tiers of gathered fabric, and several rows of rickrack were sometimes added as an embellishment. One Hopi woman related that her mother made these outfits every Fourth of July for her two daughters. They were cool and comfortable dresses for summer wear. Courtesy of the Bureau of Indian Affairs Archives, Phoenix Area Office.

education. In fact, most early educators encouraged complete separation of the children from their homes and culture. Visits from parents were discouraged if not forbidden altogether.

There was a further problem because government schools were not organized just to teach a basic education. Through the schools, vigorous attempts were made to erase every vestige of Hopi culture, language, and religion. Students were expected to wear western clothing. Their hair was cut short, and the use of their native language was met with severe punishment. It was absolutely forbidden for the students to practice any part of their traditional religion.

Vocational training was a large part of government school education. Boys were taught practical trades such as farming, carpentry, masonry, and mechanics. Girls' training leaned heavily to the domestic arts and included housekeeping, cooking and nutrition, dairying, and of course, sewing. An 1890 report to the Department of the Interior from the Commissioner of Indian Affairs listed "Rules for Indian Schools" (*Annual Reports of the Department of the Interior, Indian Affairs* 1890: CLII). Under the heading of Industrial Work the report stated that, "The girls must be systematically trained in every branch of housekeeping and in dairy work; be taught to cut, make, and mend garments for both men and women."

Some boys were taught tailoring, but it was the female students who were expected to learn to sew garments and, ultimately, to stitch all of the clothing and linens needed for the students and in the operation of the

Opposite Page. Crazy Quilt, c. 1900–1910. Ida Mae Fredericks Murdock was the first Hopi to obtain a college degree. Her parents sent her to school at Northern Arizona University in Flagstaff, Arizona, in 1935, when the institution was the state teacher's college. Ida Mae studied elementary education. One fellow student who became a good friend was Helen Reeder, a girl from the mining town of Miami, Arizona. The two young women remained close through their four years of college until their graduation in 1939.

Ida Mae recalled that she and Helen had many adventures together. On Saturdays when they were out of school, they sometimes spent the whole day climbing up to the fire lookout on top of the mountain outside of Flagstaff, returning to the campus late in the evening after dark. After graduation they both left Flagstaff to teach school. Ida Mae, a teacher all of her life, worked in Oklahoma, Nebraska, Oregon, and Arizona. Ida Mae and Helen remained friends through all of the following years, and when Helen died in 1954, her husband contacted Ida Mae and told her he wanted her to have something of Helen's as a special remembrance. He gave her an exquisite turn-of-the-century Crazy Quilt top that had been in Helen's family for many years. Ida Mae found a group of quilters to put a backing on the quilt and protect it from excessive wear.

Ida Mae cherished the quilt as an enduring symbol of her friendship with Helen. The Crazy Quilt is heavily embellished with feather stitching and embroidered designs of birds, flowers, butterflies, grasshoppers, and stars. The colors of the silks and velvets are still vivid, nearly a century after it was created, and almost half of a century after Helen's passing. The lovely quilt is a lasting memento of a special friendship between two cultures. Quilt courtesy of Ida Mae Murdock. Photography by David Elliott.

Students at the Phoenix Indian High School sewing room, c. 1950s. Courtesy of the Bureau of Indian Affairs Archives, Phoenix Area Office.

Students hand stitching linens, c. 1950s. Phoenix Indian High School. Courtesy of the Bureau of Indian Affairs Archives, Phoenix Area Office.

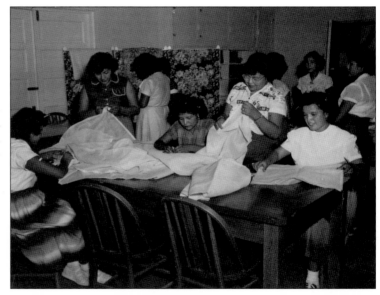

Student marking a pattern for the sewing class at the Phoenix Indian High School, c. 1950s. Courtesy of the Bureau of Indian Affairs Archives, Phoenix Area Office.

Tuba City Indian School, c. 1930s. The students dressed in uniforms and marched everywhere. Photograph courtesy of Mary May Bailey.

school. In the beginning, this was a daunting challenge for the school matrons and teachers because while the Hopi girls were very skilled in their traditional arts of making pottery and weaving baskets, they did not have a legacy of stitchery. In 1889 J. C. Baker, Superintendent of the Keams Canyon School, noted in amazed frustration that the girls had never been taught needlework. The sewing teacher wrote, "I can not learn [sic] that the children [girls] have ever been instructed in needlework" (Baker 1889: 374).

The Hopi students took to sewing very quickly, however, and three years later Superintendent Ralph P. Collins wrote in his annual report that:

> The girls show considerable efficiency in domestic work. Each girl, many only 6 or 7 years old, made herself two dresses, two skirts, and two suits of underclothes, doing all of the sewing of seams, hemming, and buttonholes by hand. They also do good mending and darning, and the larger ones will soon be able to cut garments unassisted [Collins 1892: 652-53].

Sewing and clothing construction were an important part of government education, and once the Hopi girls learned to sew they began a tradition of stitching clothing for themselves and their families that has lasted until the present. Early lesson plans for schools list in precise detail

41

the sewing skills that were expected to be taught. A 1916 edition of the *Tentative Course of Study for United States Indian Schools* contains nearly a dozen pages of sewing skills to be mastered (Sells 1916). For girls in the fourth through sixth grades, instruction began with basic pattern drafting, operation of a sewing machine, pricing materials, and construction of domestic linens, dresses, aprons, and other basic garments. Older girls were taught advanced sewing, tailoring, crochet, art needlework, embroidery, bobbin and filet lace making, and millinery.

Cotton, Anglo-style dresses became popular with many Hopi women and girls who went away to school, although some girls were criticized by their families for wearing nontraditional dress. The customary woolen *manta*, the *kanelkwasa*, was scratchy, hot in the summer, and difficult to clean. One girl who went away to boarding school recalled that she often wore a cotton dress under her *manta* when she went home during the summer break. She rolled the sleeves up so that her mother would not know she was wearing the "white man's clothes" underneath. Another quilter from a less traditional family said that when she went away to school her mother sewed an Anglo-style dress and her first slip to wear under it. She was so proud of the beautiful handwork that her mother had done on the slip that she lengthened the straps so that her slip would hang below the hem of her dress, and everyone would see what a beautiful underslip she was wearing.

Flour sacks were a common source of fabric, especially for slips and underware. Many Hopi women recall the dresses, blouses, and undergarments that their mothers stitched from flour sacks. Some of the fabric from flour and sugar sacks was printed with a design, and some was plain white with a colored logo. Vintage photographs often show Hopi men wearing loose, white pants that were sewn with fabric from those sacks.

Most older Hopi women alive today have attended the government boarding schools where they received extensive training in sewing and garment construction. Because of their early seamstress training, and because of economics and the distances from towns and convenient shopping, many still sew their dresses, aprons, skirts and shirts, and other items for their households. One Hopi woman related that her mother was a talented seamstress who could design any garment without a commercial pattern. She said that when they went to Flagstaff, Arizona, the nearest large town, she and her sister would always look in the windows of the Babbitt Brothers Trading Company. They didn't ever go in the store because they couldn't afford any of the goods, but they would point out various dresses to their mother, and just from looking at them she would later sew a copy that was "just as beautiful as the dress in the store."

Quilting, naturally, was a logical step in the process of teaching sewing. With the small seams and precision required in matching points and corners, patchwork required an additional level of stitching skills that the Hopi girls soon mastered. Furthermore, in the sewing classes there would have been an abundance of scraps and cutaways, the fabric pieces left over from the sewing of school uniforms and other garments. Putting these scraps to good use, the students soon were piecing quilts. Sarah Abbott, Field Matron for the Hopi Reservation, wrote in 1900 that, "The class in sewing has made over 500 garments—the greater part from their own material; 33 quilts have been made, 18 of which were made by returned schoolgirls" (Abbott 1900: 477).

Through the following decades sewing and quilting continued to be heavily emphasized in the Indian boarding schools. Although many contemporary Hopi quilters learned stitching skills from their mothers and grandmothers, those crafts were also reinforced year after year in the school curriculum.

Hopi women piecing quilt blocks, c. 1898–1901. Negative No. 4611. The woman at the left appears to have completed several Four Patch blocks. This turn-of-the-century photograph perhaps indicates that quilting had quickly become a social pastime outside of the quilting bees held at mission churches. The two girls in the center are wearing their hair in the distinctive butterfly whorl, a sign that they are unmarried maidens. The two women at the left and right sides are wearing their hair in the traditional style of married Hopi females. Their hair is parted in the center and pulled to the sides of their faces, and the lengths of hair are wrapped with hair and yarn. Courtesy of the California Historical Society, Title Insurance and Trust Photo Collection, Department of Special Collections, University of Southern California Library.

The Mennonite Mission at Oraibi, c. 1901. Built by Heinrich Voth and Hopi workers. Courtesy of the Mennonite Library and Archives, Bethel College, North Newton, Kansas, H. R. Voth photo.

Quilting Bees at Oraibi

Government schools were not the only places where stitching was taught to Hopi girls and women. In the 1800s, Christian missionaries began arriving in the Hopi villages, and sewing and quilting bees were an important component of their evangelizing efforts. Heinrich and Martha Voth were Mennonite missionaries who were sent to Oraibi in 1893. They both, immediately, set out to learn the Hopi language with the ultimate goal of translating scriptures and hymns into the native tongue. Heinrich Voth held street meetings several times each week, preaching the gospel to any who would listen. The Voths carried a small, portable organ and set it up in the open plazas, where Mrs. Voth played music and sang hymns.

By the fall of their first year on Third Mesa, Martha was holding "sewing club" meetings. Her diaries, now archived at Bethel College in North Newton, Kansas, contain numerous references to the sewing club and quilting bee activities. In early December 1893 there was a shipment of donated fabrics and sewing supplies. The Hopi women were very excited about the arrival of the new materials. On December 4, Martha recorded in her journal, "Since the Indians heard about our getting the things for the sewing club the other day, they virtually inundated us today. Everyone wanted to have something." Martha began holding frequent bees, and later references in her journals mention the Hopi ladies sewing "pieces of quilt."

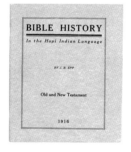

Bible History in pamphlet form, 1916, 106 pages. Translated into Hopi by Mennonite missionary J. B. Epp. Courtesy of Edison and Karen Tootsie.

Hopi women in Martha Voth's sewing class at the Mennonite Mission at Oraibi, c. 1890s. The mothers sewed western-style dresses for their daughters. Courtesy of the Mennonite Library and Archives, Bethel College, North Newton, Kansas, H. R. Voth photo.

Within a year of their arrival on the Hopi mesas, Martha wrote to *The Indian's Friend*, the monthly magazine of The Women's National Indian Association, that she and Mr. Voth could speak "the Oreiba language" quite fluently. She went on in that February 1894 issue to relate a humorous incident pertaining to teaching sewing to women, in a culture where only men traditionally practiced that skill. Martha wrote:

> As among these people, the Moquis, as the men do most of the sewing I have commenced to teach the women. They have gathered twice in our house, and did quite well for the first time, although it appeared difficult for them. Some brought their long five and six inch needles, which they use to darn their blankets with. Their clumsy efforts caused a great deal of merriment, though they seem willing to learn.
>
> The men thought it very funny that the women should learn to sew, and asked Mr. Voth, who went that day to Oreiba how the women were getting along [Voth 1894: 6].

Martha pointed out that her bees did have one unusual aspect. When the women arrived at her house to sew, she seated them on chairs and benches about the room. But the Hopis were more accustomed to sitting on the floor, and soon "one after another slipped down from her seat,

Shadowbox Quilt, 78" x 71", 1996. Pieced from White Cross blocks by Pearl Nuvangyaoma, Shipaulovi. Photography by David Elliott.

Quilting bee at Bacavi Mennonite Church, c. 1950s. Photograph courtesy of the Mennonite Library and Archives, Bethel College, North Newton, Kansas.

Bacavi quilter showing her pieced quilt top, c. 1950s. Photograph courtesy of the Mennonite Library and Archives, Bethel College, North Newton, Kansas.

Quilting bee at Oraibi Mennonite Church, 1893. Missionary Martha Voth is standing at the table sorting through pieces of fabric. Courtesy of the Mennonite Library and Archives, Bethel College, North Newton, Kansas, H. R. Voth photo #93.

Quilting bee at Oraibi Mennonite Church, 1893. Missionary Martha Voth is standing at the right and wearing a sun-bonnet. Courtesy of the Mennonite Library and Archives, Bethel College, North Newton, Kansas, H. R. Voth photo #95.

until finally only one remained sitting in her chair. They made themselves quite at home." Whether seated on a chair or a dirt floor, the Hopi women took to quilting as though they had been doing it forever. Since those years in the late 1800s there have been weekly quilting bees held almost without interruption on Third Mesa.

Heinrich and Martha built a mission house on the desert floor about two miles from the base of Third Mesa and Oraibi. Sadly, in the spring of 1901, Martha and her newborn infant died. She and her baby were buried in a sandy grave near the mission home. Later that year construction of the mission church was completed. The church was built up on the edge of the mesa on the outskirts of Oraibi. Four decades later the building was hit by lightning and most of the structure burned to the ground. Today, as one ascends the highway to Third Mesa, the skeletal walls of the church and bell tower still are etched along the mesa skyline, a silent reminder of the meeting of two cultures.

Voth left mission work shortly after Martha's death, but her efforts were carried on by the wives of subsequent Mennonite missionaries. Mrs. J. B. Epp, who began her work at Hopi in the first years of this century, organized quilting bees and "in these the opportunity was abundantly granted to speak of the great Physician of souls" (Frey 1915: 25).

Another interesting tool, adapted as a means of spreading the message of the Bible, was a stereopticon show with slides used by Mr. and Mrs. J. B. Frey, who were later Mennonite missionaries at Oraibi. The Freys held night meetings in the village streets and showed images of Bible scenes on a white sheet hung from a wall. When the wind blew, the

As part of the missionary outreach, Martha Voth set up her portable organ in the village streets at Oraibi, c. 1890s. Her music and singing attracted many who sometimes stayed to hear a sermon. Courtesy of the Mennonite Library and Archives, Bethel College, North Newton, Kansas, H. R. Voth photo.

Mennonite missionary Heinrich Voth preaching a sermon in the streets of Oraibi, c. 1890s. Courtesy of the Mennonite Library and Archives, Bethel College, North Newton, Kansas, H. R. Voth photo.

figures projected on the sheet seemed to move, and as Frey told Bible stories it was an amazing entertainment for the Hopis sitting around the plaza "wrapped in shawls and quilts" (Johnson 1933: 135).

Mennonite missionaries have labored among the Hopis for over a century, but it has never been easy nor fruitful work. Two decades after he left Arizona, Voth stated that the Hopi reservation was "one of the most difficult of mission fields" (Wright 1979: 2). At that time the Third Mesa church numbered only a few dozen souls, just over one convert per year.

Quilting was always a natural device for missionary work. The Hopi women, eager to learn more sewing and piecing techniques, returned to the mission each week. And in the quiet hours of stitching and piecing, a missionary could turn the talk to the gospel and to following what some Hopis called "the Jesus road." Louise A. Young was a Hopi missionary at First Mesa. In 1896 she wrote of her heavy reliance on sewing bees and quilting to spread the word among the people. Every Saturday morning she taught sewing to the young girls, even though "most of them have never had a needle in hand before" (Young 1896: 8).

On Mondays and Thursdays Miss Young held sewing bees for the women. In her letter to *The Indian's Friend*, she wrote that at the last bee they had forty people, and they stayed all day to sew. There were "twenty-four who sewed, twelve were children mostly too young to walk, and the rest were men." Men of course, often participated in the sewing bees; they were the ones with the long tradition of weaving and sewing, arts that still are practiced today by many Hopi men. Furthermore, it is not uncommon for Hopi men to make quilts.

Miss Young's bees must have been noisy affairs with all of the children in attendance. She noted that there were "babies on the right of us, babies on the left of us and sleeping babies were rolled in their blankets or tied in their cradles and deposited under the table." But she felt that everyone greatly enjoyed the gatherings, and there was always a lot of visiting and joking.

Indeed, quilting bees are still popular proselytizing activities among the missionaries. One retired church worker recalled that in her first weeks of eager service at a Moencopi church she gave out all of the donated fabric and sewing supplies at one quilting bee. The bewildered young woman was chastised for her over-generous actions, but she soon learned that with enough fabric to finish their quilts, the Hopi ladies stayed away from the church until they ran out of cloth. At future bees the young worker sparingly handed out supplies, guaranteeing that the women would return each week to hear more gospel lessons—and for more fabric to piece their quilt blocks (interview with Pearl Jensen, 1996).

There were many hardships for missionaries living in a remote area, far from conveniences, schools, and medical care. Just as the Voths lost a child, Mr. and Mrs. Frey also buried a child near their mission church at Moencopi. It was a difficult life for missionaries and Hopis alike, but 1918

Hopi quilters at Moencopi with a pieced quilt top, c. 1970s. Photograph courtesy of Grace Jensen.

Kachinas and Calico Quilt by Susie Archambeau, 41" x 55", 1996. The kachina faces on this quilt were painted by eighty-nine-year-old Susie Archambeau. The painted blocks are set with purple calico fabric, an interesting blending of a traditional quilting fabric with Hopi imagery. Photography by David Elliott.

brought even more trouble in the form of smallpox and the terrible influenza epidemic that left few families untouched.

In April 1918 Maria Schirmer, the Mennonite missionary at Hotevilla, wrote to the Missionary Board that all of the mesa villages had been afflicted with smallpox for several months. Fortunately, there had been no deaths at Hotevilla, and life was getting back to normal. There had been no home visits because of the quarantine, but the "sewing days are still well attended and I trust will not remain without results" (Schirmer 1918).

Maria Schirmer went to Third Mesa in 1906. She was the first missionary at Hotevilla, and she spent most the of next three decades working on the Hopi mesas. Partly as a result of the terrible epidemics, such as the one that devastated many villages in 1918, Maria eventually adopted and raised four orphaned Hopi children. Maria relied heavily on music to aid her missionary activities, and she translated many favorite hymns into Hopi. But the weekly quilting bees at her Mennonite mission church were always the best attended events, and the most effective of her proselytizing activities.

John and Mabel Suderman were missionaries at Oraibi in the 1930s. They wrote monthly newsletters to the "Mission Friends of the Hopi Indians." As with the efforts of the earlier missionaries, sewing classes were the most popular activities that were held at the church. Mrs. Suderman's Thursday afternoon Women's Sewing Class had an average attendance of 40 to 60 women, although the majority of them were "unsaved." She stated quite frankly in her January 1938 newsletter that most of the women come to the quilting bees "because of the patches." And she made a plea for the mission supporters to send more fabric patches "size 4x6 and 4x4."

Quilting bee at Oraibi Mennonite Church, 1893. Martha Voth is pouring water so that one of the quilters can wash her hands before she begins working with the fabric. Courtesy of the Mennonite Library and Archives, Bethel College, North Newton Kansas, H. R. Voth photo #94.

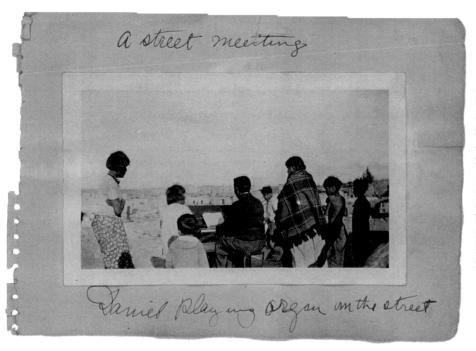

a street meeting

Daniel playing organ on the street

A street meeting, Daniel Schirmer playing the organ, c. 1940s. Daniel Schirmer was a Hopi child adopted by Maria Schirmer, a Mennonite missionary at Hotevilla, after his parents died in an epidemic. Daniel later became a preacher. Photograph courtesy of Mary Martha Baumgartner.

In her April 1938 newsletter, Mrs. Suderman thanked all the "dear ladies of the Mission societies" for sending patches, needles, and thread. And she stated that the quilting bees are still "one of the best means of giving the gospel to unsaved women." She went on to describe a recent quilting bee attended by twenty-eight women, all of whom sat on the floor to do their piecing. Partway through the afternoon she would ask them all to stop sewing to sing some hymns and listen to Bible stories. As she would read to them she knew that some were listening, but more were "thinking about their patches."

Mrs. Suderman also wrote about what she called the Hopi women's "honorable hands." She had noticed that when the women came to her sewing classes, many of them had not washed their hands. In the beginning she had been tempted to ask them to wash before they started to sew. Later, she learned that when a Hopi woman went out in public she would often leave a bit of dough and flour on her hands. This indicated to others that she had been busy working and was not lazy. Mrs. Suderman referred to this as "honorable hands."

Maria Schirmer holding her adopted Hopi daughter, Mary Martha, 1940. Mary Martha was the youngest of four Hopi children adopted by Maria Schirmer. Photograph courtesy of Mary Martha Baumgartner.

Sunlight Mission and the mission house at Second Mesa, 1928. Photography courtesy of Eleanor Means Hull.

Sunlight Mission

In 1898 Abigail Johnson graduated from the Baptist Missionary Training School in Chicago, Illinois. She was first sent to work among the Cheyennes and Arapahos, replacing a missionary woman who had been stricken with typhoid fever. Late in 1901 Miss Johnson was transferred to the Hopi Reservation, where she established a mission with her coworker, Miss Ida Schofield. Through the assistance of Sarah Abbott, the Field Matron, they found a house in Polacca at the base of First Mesa.

Like Heinrich and Martha Voth, Miss Johnson realized that she would have to learn to speak the Hopi language in order to work among them effectively. For a time she rode a horse all the way to Third Mesa to study with the Mennonites, but she soon gave that up because of the distance and her busy schedule. Eventually, she became fluent in Hopi and wrote a small grammar that included some of her favorite hymns translated into Hopi.

Abigail Johnson spent most of her adult life among the Hopi people. Her missionary work was her primary vocation, but she was also a friend who offered her help when it was needed. Miss Johnson believed that Christianity was the only path to save the souls of the Hopi people. In the biography of her life, *Sunlight on the Hopi Mesas* by Florence Crannell Means, there is an often quoted passage that reveals the depth of feeling

Members of the summer vacation bible school at the Sunlight Mission, 1928. Miss Abigail Johnson and Miss Flint at left. Photograph courtesy of Eleanor Means Hull.

Strip Quilt Variation by Jessie Mae Quotskuyva, 70" x 68", c. 1950s. Jessie Mae hand pieced her quilt top with every piece of fabric available in her scrap bag. This colorful top contains quilt blocks of cotton, satin, corduroy, flannel, flour sacking, curtain and upholstery fabric, piqué, and brocade. In the center of the bottom row there is even a tiny, hand pieced eight-pointed star block. For some of the piecing Jessie Mae used a double strand of white thread, for the rest of the top she used black.

Janice Dennis was given the quilt top, along with a bag of hand pieced star blocks, several years ago when Jessie Mae passed away. Janice is a quilter, and she is stitching the star blocks into a quilt top in memory of her clan relative, Jessie Mae Quotskuyva. Quilt courtesy of Janice Dennis. Photography by David Elliott.

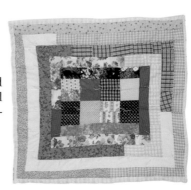

Crazy Quilt, 1966. Baby quilt pieced from White Cross blocks by Pearl Nuvangyaoma, Shipaulovi. Photography by David Elliott.

Miriam Torivio with one of her bright pieced and tied quilts, 1996, Sunlight Mission, Second Mesa.

she held for her missionary work. Referring to the sacred masks and other religious objects that she saw in many Hopi homes it was recorded that:

> Miss Johnson thrilled with horror as she looked at the very tools of a false religion. Later missionaries, with a broader knowledge of comparative religion, might see in these tools a blind approach to the one God. Miss Johnson experienced only repugnance, together with a great thankfulness that she was privileged to bring light into such darkness [Means 1960: 59].

In spite of her strong aversion to Hopi religion, however, Abigail Johnson also felt a genuine respect for the Hopi people. Miss Johnson formed an especially close friendship with one Hopi woman who eventually adopted her. Mother Poboly held a naming ceremony, even washing Abigail's hair with traditional yucca root soap. She was given the name of *Sikyanapi,* Yellow Leaf, and adopted into the Mustard Clan (Means 1960: 64).

Miss Johnson and other "mission Marys," as they were sometimes called by the Hopis (who made that natural connection from the word "missionary"), continued the evangelizing work. Like the Voths, they held street meetings, and carried a portable organ up the trail to the villages on the mesa top where they preached the gospel and played hymns in the open air. Abigail also played the guitar and the Hopis enjoyed hearing her sing. One difficulty, however, was that her small voice did not carry far. Consequently, she implemented the use of a megaphone in her sermons. At first she made them from cardboard, but eventually she was able to purchase a real megaphone, an instrument that she felt was a great aid in her work among the Hopis (Means 1960: 83).

At Polacca, Miss Johnson organized sewing and quilting bees as the Mennonites had done at Third Mesa. Sarah Abbott had already been teaching the women to sew, and many of the Hopi women had changed from wearing the heavy, traditional woolen dresses, or *mantas*, to the lighter, cotton dresses.

When the missionaries corresponded with friends and their home churches, the items that they always requested were yard goods and sewing supplies. One source for quilting patches was the White Cross Blocks that were sent to the Indian missions. For decades urban women from Mennonite and Baptist churches around the country have had a tradition of cutting postcard-sized quilt blocks of fabric scraps, known as White Cross Blocks. These blocks were then piled into stacks of one hundred pieces and tied into bundles with string. Each set of one hundred squares might have many matching pieces, or they could be of a wide assortment of colors and patterns. It was a great challenge for the Hopi women to piece together an attractive quilt top from the wildly unmatched fabrics.

For the Christian ladies around the country, gathering to cut the quilt blocks was a favorite social activity, as well as a charitable way to share what they could. From Halstead, Kansas, the local newspaper, *The Independent*, reported that, "The Dorcas [Mission] Society of the Mennonite church, met last Thursday for an all day meeting in the Church basement. At noon a covered dish luncheon was served. Quilt blocks for the Arizona and Montana Mission field were cut" (11/26/37). During World War II, the Dorcas Mission Society reported: "fifty-two garments were sewed and sent to relief. Bed sheets are given to church boys going to camp. Money was sent to Home, Foreign, and other

Miss Abigail Johnson, Baptist missionary at Second Mesa, 1928. Miss Johnson held weekly quilting bees for Hopi men and women. Photograph courtesy of Eleanor Means Hull.

"Pliny's limousine." The wagon was used by Pliny Adams when he offered rides to the mission to attend church services and quilting bees, 1928. Photograph courtesy of Eleanor Means Hull.

Quilting bee at Bacavi Mennonite Church, c. 1950s. Photograph courtesy of the Mennonite Library and Archives, Bethel College, North Newton, Kansas.

mission stations, and the pension fund. Quilt patches were sent to Arizona and Montana stations" (6/19/42).

Florence Crannell Means, Miss Johnson's friend and biographer, wrote of the quilting bees held at the mission church:

> Such assemblages have been effective with Indian women of all tribes. The something-for-nothing quilt blocks, post-card size, which church women for generations have cut and sent, may have been the opening wedge, but sociability followed close behind. Those who came were seldom averse to hearing Bible stories and a Bible message, and most of them liked to join in the hymns. The community effort was pleasant to them, akin to their own work parties. It was an occasion, when the pieced top, with the cotton batting and calico lining paid for by an individual, was stretched out for tying or, less often, for quilting. Church pews made a workable support for the quilting frame [Means 1960: 108].

Florence Means visited Abigail Johnson several times while she was collecting material for her extensive writings. In her 1928 diary, Mrs. Means wrote of her trip from her home in Colorado to the Hopi country, and about sewing at the church. On February 17, she noted: "Friday. The

Appliqué Flower top by Luella Burton, 74" x 60", c. 1930s. The flowers and flower pots on each block of this quilt were hand appliquéd, and each piece was outlined with black buttonhole stitching. Many of the flowers were cut from flour sack fabric, and each flower has a round, yellow center. The quilt top is entirely hand pieced with the blocks set on point. Alternate setting blocks and the outer border are pieced from the vintage "Nile green" fabric that was commonly used in quilts in the late 1920s and 1930s.

The owner of the quilt top is Eileen Randolph who recalled that her Aunt Luella was an accomplished quiltmaker, and in her lifetime she made many quilts. Quilt top courtesy of Eileen Randolph. Photography by David Elliott.

Spool Baby Quilt, 42" x 41", 1995. Hand pieced and tied by Rita Nuvangyaoma, Shipaulovi. Photography by David Elliott.

women came down from the Mesa to sewing at the church—*most fascinating*: buckskin moccasins, papooses, women sitting on floor, etc." The following day, on Saturday afternoon when there was no school, Miss Johnson held sewing bees for the young people (Means 1928).

Quilting bees were not always looked upon as being innocuous, however. The missionaries and their converts were often ridiculed or threatened by traditional Hopis, and as peaceful as the Hopi people are, there were times of danger for the Christians. In her autobiography, Abigail Johnson tells of a confrontation with a traditional Hopi man at a quilting bee. He was clearly distressed because his daughter was a convert to Christianity. He came to a quilting bee that was also being attended by several missionaries, and declared that the missionaries had caused the Hopi people a great deal of trouble.

The old man referred back to the times when the Catholic Padres had forced religion upon the Hopis who had been forced to kill the priests in order to be able to practice their traditional religion. That was the only right way for the Hopis. Then, motioning to the "colorful pieces the women were sewing together," he said, "Of course these things are all

Before roads were built to the mesa tops, the stone stairways were the only access to the Hopi villages. These are the stone steps of the south stairway to Shipaulovi, 1923. Courtesy of C. Burton Cosgrove.

right, but you must not listen to the things they are telling you about for it belongs to *Nukpana* (the devil)" (Johnson 1933: 149).

Abigail Johnson had worked at First Mesa for twenty years when she left for California for a time because of poor health. In 1923 she applied to return to the Hopi mission field, and was assigned to the more remote Sunlight Mission on Second Mesa. Here she resumed her sewing classes and quilting bees, but she also instituted, with the help of Hopi convert Pliny Adams, sewing meetings for men.

The Hopi men were, of course, "good needlemen." They had a generations-old tradition of spinning, weaving, sewing, knitting, and embroidery. Naturally, the men's quilting bees proved to be very popular at Sunlight Mission Church, and many of today's Hopi quilters recall their fathers and grandfathers who went to the mission for the bees. One Second Mesa quilter reminisced that there were night classes for the men. They stitched quilts from old clothes and suits, sometimes in squares and sometimes in a Crazy Quilt pattern.

For many years, one quilter cherished the quilt that had been made by her father. It was a Crazy Quilt stitched of heavy woolen fabrics cut from old clothing. Each piece of the quilt was sewn with a border of embroidery stitches done in red thread. Eventually the quilt became threadbare from use and was discarded.

Edison Tootsie's father was also one of the quilters. Edison recalls going to the quiltings with his father when he was a small child. Mr. Tootsie would take his wagon around and give rides to all of the men who wanted to go to the mission to quilt. They would stay all day to sew.

Trading post at Second Mesa, c. 1940s. The trading post is the stone building at the left. On top of the mesa are the villages of Mishongnovi and Shipaulovi. Photograph courtesy of Mary Martha Baumgartner.

Their quilts were heavy, the pieces were cut from worn out wool suits and denim.

During the Depression, when supplies were difficult to come by, needles were hand made by straightening the keys that were attached to cans of Arbuckles Coffee. The curved handle part was straightened and a point was made on the end. The opposite end that was used to twist open the metal ring on the can was threaded with string or yarn. This made a heavy, but serviceable, needle for stitching quilt blocks or tying the layers of a top, batting, and lining together. (Innovative Hopi girls unrolled the strips of tin from the key and used them to roll up their long, dark hair. When their hair was dry, the tin strips were unrolled, leaving soft waves and curls.)

Edison also recalled that the men would gather at the Polacca Day School to make mattresses. They used heavy ticking fabric for the covering, and the inside would be stuffed with raw cotton. Along the sides they made a rolled edge that was sewn with a stitch used in making saddles. Two of the heavy coffee can needles, threaded with heavy string, were used to make a running stitch, like a figure eight, that secured the edges of the mattresses.

Another interesting account of a Hopi man doing fine needlework comes from the honeymoon diary kept by Emma Walmisley Sykes, who spent some time at the Keams Canyon Trading Post. In the summer of 1895 Emma and her husband, Godfrey, were married in England and traveled across the Atlantic Ocean, and then west to Keams Canyon on the eastern edge of the Hopi reservation. Sykes had been hired to manage the trading post for several months while his friend, Thomas Keam, traveled back to England to visit his family.

Emma employed a Hopi girl to do the housecleaning, and an elderly Hopi man who had been given the western name of Horace Greeley to do

Crazy Quilt top by Betty Poley, 77" x 57", c. 1950s. Quilt top foundation pieced on muslin blocks with silk and satin fabrics and machine top-stitched. Eileen Randolph, owner of the Crazy Quilt top, related that her mother was a fine seamstress. She told her daughter that when it came to stitchery, "fix it for yourself and it will last forever." Quilt courtesy of Eileen Randolph. Photography by David Elliott.

Trip Around the World Quilt by Frieda Yoyhoeoma of Shipaulovi, 1996. Frieda hand quilted this striking quilt pieced with purple prints and a solid white fabric. The use of only two main colors gives the quilt a strong geometric effect, reminiscent of the streaks of lightning often seen in Hopi design.

the laundry. Because of his sewing skills, Greeley also did some household sewing for Mrs. Sykes. In a July entry Emma recorded in her journal that, "Old Horace Greeley sat near us on the verandah, making us two new large pillows; they are stuffed with wool. He had to card the wool first, the process interested me. I made the slips and he sewed them up so neatly" (Boyer and Lowell 1989: 440).

Abigail Johnson stayed on at the Sunlight Mission through the Depression years. She retired in 1938, but returned for visits and to stay for a time in 1946 when she was well into her seventies. New missionaries labor at the Second Mesa church today, and the quilting bees continue, one hundred years after the arrival of the first Baptist "mission Marys."

Oraibi village on Third Mesa has been continuously inhabited since A. D. 1150. This photograph shows the view to the southwest, 1923. Courtesy of C. Burton Cosgrove.

The Mormons and the Lamanites

The Church of Jesus Christ of Latter-day Saints has always had an interest in Native Americans. Mormons regard them as Israelites (known as Lamanites to the Mormons in this country), one of the Lost Tribes who had come to this continent from Jerusalem, centuries before the time of Christ. Mormons believe the Indians are the "genuine children of Biblical Israel" (Flake 1965: 3). Furthermore, the *Book of Mormon*, the volumes of scripture that are regarded by the Mormons as equally important to their religion as the Bible, is essentially the history of the ancestors of the Native Americans on this continent.

Ester Batala of Mishongnovi on Second Mesa, 1964. Piled behind Mrs. Batala is a stack of folded blankets and patchwork quilts. Courtesy of the Museum of Northern Arizona.

"Moen Copie Woolen Mill—First and Only One in Arizona." The woolen mill was built in 1879 by John W. Young. Used by permission of the University of Arizona Press. (See McClintock.)

The Mormons always looked upon Native Americans as their brethren, and made every attempt to befriend and aid them. The Mormon prophet, Brigham Young, created the Southern Indian Mission in 1854, and appointed Jacob Hamblin "Apostle to the Lamanites" as mission president in 1857. During the 1800s many Indian children in the West were victims of the Indian slave traffic. In order to save as many children as possible from a life of slavery, Brigham Young advised church members to "buy up the Lamanite children as fast as they could, and educate them and teach them the gospel, so that many generations would not pass ere they should become a white and delightsome people" (Brooks 1944: 6).

The Mormons admired the Hopis and greatly respected their agricultural abilities. A measure of their respect can be seen in their repeated attempts to persuade the Hopis to move to Utah and live beside the Mormons. Because the Hopis were known to be a peaceful people, many Mormon leaders thought that through relocation to the Great Basin country, they could offer protection to the Hopis. Although a few Hopis did visit Salt Lake City, they were never tempted to leave their traditional homelands.

Jacob Hamblin and some companions made their first visit to the Hopi country in 1858. They were very impressed with the Hopi people, and immediately saw correlations between kiva rituals and Mormon temple ceremonies, a sedentary agricultural tradition, and textile skills.

Painted Pottery Quilt by Bonnie Chapella, 43" x 35", 1996. Bonnie has set her painted quilt blocks with strip pieced sashing. A turquoise border adds a touch of color that effectively frames the entire quilt. Photography by David Elliott.

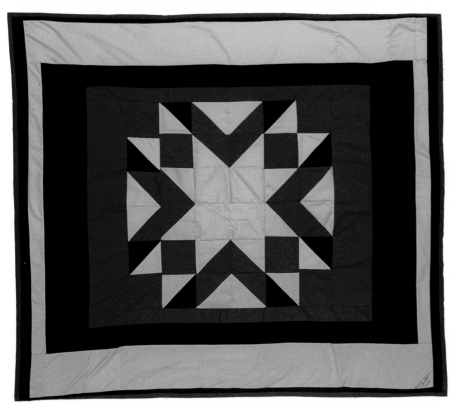

Variable Star Medallion Quilt by Krisenda Lonnie, 54" x 60", 1996. Krisenda is a Second Mesa quilter. She machine pieced her Variable Star Quilt of maroon and gold solids. Photography by David Elliott.

Hamblin and his group of missionaries made several more trips to the mesa country over the following years.

In addition to rescuing Native American children from a life of slavery, Brigham Young also recommended that missionaries marry Indian women "as a means of cementing the friendship between the races" (Brooks 1944: 28). In 1864 Hamblin was advised by Brigham Young that the missionaries were at liberty to marry "Moqui girls" (Brooks 1944: 32). Because polygamy was practiced in the Mormon church during the nineteenth century, men who were already married were encouraged to secure the agreement of their first wives before they took additional wives. Nevertheless, when Mormon historian Juanita Brooks did extensive research on Mormon and Indian relations, she did not record any marriages between missionaries and Hopi women. Perhaps one reason for the lack of intermarriage between Mormons and Hopis is that the Hopi people are monogamous, and they looked with disfavor on the Mormon system of plural marriage.

Although many found the Hopi country to be a dreary wasteland, there were some visitors who were quite enchanted with the region. Mormon missionary C. L. Christensen called the Hopi houses on the mesa tops "castles." The house walls were plastered with a native white

A Hopi woman is using a patchwork quilt top as a *momokpi*, a carrying bag worn over the shoulder, c. 1905–1912. Courtesy of the Kate Cory Collection, Museum of Northern Arizona.

Hopi bride and groom posing in front of several hanging blankets, sashes, and a pieced Nine Patch Quilt. The Hopi woman is wearing a *manta*, a traditional dress, a tube-like woolen garment that secures over one shoulder. Negative No. 27653. Courtesy of the Arizona Historical Society.

clay and "from a distance they glitter in the sun and look beautiful" (Christensen 1922).

Christensen was most impressed by the industrious nature of the Hopis. He described watching the Hopi women each morning going down to the springs below the mesa to collect the day's supply of water in their pottery jugs. Even though they balanced the heavy, water-filled ollas on their heads as they climbed the steep stairway, they called happy greetings as they passed their neighbors. He told of the distances that the men and children ran each day, and of their subsequent good health. And, somewhat surprisingly in view of his role as a missionary, he described the devoted manner in which they gave thanks each day to "the Great Creator."

One interesting motive for a subsequent visit by Mormon missionaries to the mesas was to verify a report from John D. Lee that the Hopi language was related to Gaelic, and that the Hopi people were possibly of Welsh descent. There was an old myth that spoke of elusive Welsh Indians, and it was thought that perhaps the light-skinned Hopis might be descendants of those people. As one Mormon historian noted, "To some, scriptural promises appeared to be partially fulfilled in the Hopis" (Peterson 1973: 194). Welshman James Davis was appointed to accompany the 1858 mission as an interpreter. It was eventually decided,

Village Plaza, 65" x 54", corduroy quilt by Margaret Pacheco, Second
Mesa, 1997.

Pearl Nuvangyaoma with one of her pieced and tied baby quilts, 1996, Second Mesa.

however, that there was no scientific basis for this report (Peterson 1971: 188).

The Mormon missionaries repeatedly tried to induce the Hopis to move to Utah. On each trip they invited Hopis to return with them for a visit. On their fourth trip in 1862 they persuaded three Hopi men to visit Utah, even though the journey would require them to cross the Colorado River, an action that up to that time would not have been attempted by any Hopi person because such a crossing would go against a time-honored tradition (Flake 1965: 29). Three Mormon missionaries were left behind at Hopi, while in Utah the Hopi men toured farms and visited Prophet Brigham Young in Salt Lake City. Still, the Mormons could not tempt any Hopis to leave their homeland, in spite of the description of their environment given by missionary Thales Haskell, one of those left behind at the Hopi mesas. Haskell commented that in "the wide world over I do not believe a more bleak, lonesome, heartsickening place could be found on the earth where human beings dwell" (Flake 1965: 23).

In the early 1870s a Hopi leader named Tuba, and his wife, Katsinmana, became the first Mormon converts. In 1875 they spent a year in Utah and, two years later the couple went through the Mormon temple in St. George, Utah. They were the first Native Americans to participate in this sacred ritual. In Washington, Utah, a small settlement near St. George, Tuba and his wife saw a spinning mill that greatly interested them as they both realized the great amount of work a spinning mill could save the Hopis who were still doing all of their cotton and wool production by hand. Consequently, the Mormons were welcomed when they established a small settlement at Tuba City near Moencopi and on the western boundary of Hopi country.

In 1879, John W. Young, one of the prophet Brigham Young's sons, built the Moen Copi Woolen Mill. The Mormon settlement at Tuba City was about two miles to the south, but there was a more reliable source of water near Moencopi where Young erected his mill. The stone building boasted 192 spindles and, initially, the milling operation was a success. The problem, however, came in distribution. Located so far from towns or shipping centers, the products could not be profitably transported. Eventually the business failed, the mill was abandoned, and the stones of the building were removed and used for construction in Tuba City. The machinery was said to have been taken to St. Johns, Arizona (McClintock 1985: 158-59). A few years later the area around Tuba City was declared Navajo Reservation land, and the Mormons were forced to leave the region.

Mormons did colonize other parts of Arizona, most notably the area along the Little Colorado River just south of the Hopi mesas. This land proved to be so inhospitable, however, that the Mormon settlers struggled just to survive. As a consequence, most efforts toward missionary work among the Hopis was put on hold for nearly the next seventy years, until the second half of the twentieth century. In addition to the problems related to colonization, increasing persecution of polygamists focused Mormon energies in other directions.

However, during the following decades some individuals kept the missionary work alive among the Hopis, and in 1938 the mission field was divided into two districts, Hopi and Navajo. In that same year the first Mormon woman, Sister Lois H. Gardner, was called to missionary work (Flake 1965: 107). Through the efforts of Sister Gardner and other female missionary workers, the Relief Society, the women's organization of the Church of Jesus Christ of Latter-day Saints, was organized in several Hopi villages.

Quilting was an integral part of the Relief Society meetings. By the 1950s, there were Relief Societies organized in villages at each mesa and also at Moencopi. In the Relief Society records in the church archives, quilting activities are frequently mentioned. In 1954 the Polacca group made ten quilts during their meetings, and the following year it was recorded that they made ten quilts and eight quilt tops. The local Relief Societies held annual bazaars as fund raisers, and quilts for babies as well as full-sized quilts for beds were common items produced in the meetings to be sold at the bazaars (*Southwest Indian Mission Records Relief Society Annual Report* 1954).

One Relief Society mission president recorded her frustration with trying to hold formal meetings that started on the hour and followed a formal agenda. The Hopi women, unused to urban timetables, walked to the meetings and arrived when they could. The missionary, in frustration, handed out alarm clocks in the hope that her meetings could start on time

The Museum of Northern Arizona held the first Hopi Craftsman Show in 1930. Since that time it has been a popular annual exhibit. This photograph from an early 1930s show features some of the woven garments entered in the exhibit. On the left is a woven tapestry with an embroidered geometric design. The narrow white sash or belt features the traditional long fringe. This belt would have earned its maker a first prize of $3.00. On the top right is a traditional blanket woven of strips of rabbit fur, and on the lower right is a black-and-white woven blanket. Courtesy of the Museum of Northern Arizona.

This 1957 photograph of Vivian Earl of Sichomovi was intended to show her pottery. What is also apparent is that she was a stitcher because she is seated in front of her Singer treadle sewing machine. Courtesy of the Museum of Northern Arizona.

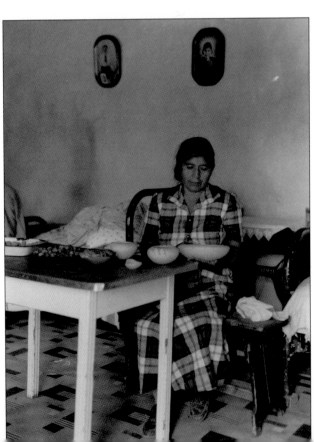

Octagons by Pearl Nuvangyaoma, 50" x 53", 1997. Pearl Nuvangyaoma hand pieced her Octagon Quilt with 171 four-inch octagons set with two-inch white squares. The quilt top is tied with a single strand of light green yarn. Although Pearl just used scrap fabrics from her sewing bag, the positioning of light and dark octagons across the face of the quilt gives it a dynamic feeling of contained movement. Photograpy by David Elliott.

and be run in what she considered an orderly fashion. When that hope failed to materialize, she yielded, and eventually became a bit less rigid in her expectations for organizing the Relief Society meetings (*Southwest Indian Mission Records Relief Society Annual Report* 1959).

All types of sewing were done at the Relief Society meetings. The ladies sewed clothing and linens for their homes, and practical instruction was given in "making over clothing." Great quantities of secondhand clothes were always given to the reservation churches to be redistributed. Many items were out of style or didn't fit. Consequently, the missionaries taught the Hopi women to remake the donated clothing into attractive, well-fitting garments. Reconstructing clothing is a lost art

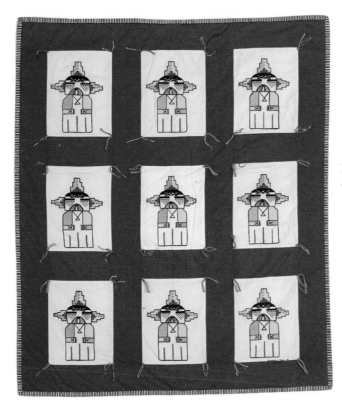

Kachina Quilt by Imogene Tewa, 45" x 38", 1997.

today, but in earlier times when home sewing was a practical alternative to commercially produced garments, it was a commonplace and very necessary talent.

Clothes that weren't used for wearing were ripped or cut apart to become patches for quilts. Donated clothing boxes at the mission churches are still a great source for scrap fabric for Hopi quilts. Relief Society annual reports often list activities such as "Ripping old clothes for Quilting" (*Southwest Indian Mission Records Relief Society Annual Report* 1952), and "Cutting quilt blocks" (*Southwest Indian Mission Records Relief Society Annual Report* 1953). Another practical use for the secondhand clothing was as filler or batting for the inside of the quilts. One quilter from Third Mesa described how she went through the boxes searching for old pants. When the seams were undone, the fronts and backs could be laid top-to-bottom to form a nicely fitting filler for a quilt.

These bulky quilts were generally just tied, not hand quilted, but they made warm covers to protect against freezing winter nights in the mesa villages. Shirts and dresses made a less desirable filler, since they didn't lie as flat, but the resourceful Hopi quilters still used every bit of fabric that came their way. Other quilters described cutting out large square pieces of fabric from old woolen coats and suits. These squares were also stitched together to become the filler for tied quilts.

In 1954 the mission president wrote in her annual report that among the Hopi women "their first love is making quilts." She felt that each meeting had to have some quilting, with only a brief theology lesson, if they hoped to continue to attract the ladies to Relief Society meetings. She added, "they want to sew always" (*Southwest Indian Mission Records Relief Society Annual Report* 1954).

Subsequent annual reports often referred to the Hopis' fondness of quiltmaking. In 1959 the new mission president noted that the Hopi women "love to make quilts" (*Southwest Indian Mission Records Relief Society Annual Report* 1959).

Singing, cooking, and homemaking instructions were also included in the lesson plans. At the Polacca Branch a group of Singing Mothers was organized, who sang at meetings and funerals. The Hopi ladies also joined with other Relief Society groups to compile a Southwest Indian cookbook. Contributing groups in addition to the Hopis were Laguna, Isleta, and Zuni pueblos as well as Apache, Navajo, and Pima. But the ongoing activity, and the greatest attraction to the women's meetings was always quilting.

In the end, in spite of 150 years of missionary contact, some historians feel that the Mormons' Hopi mission had very little impact on the Hopi people. Conversion rates, as with other denominations, remained low. The Hopis, however, perhaps had a greater influence on the Mormons. Utah historian Charles Peterson noted that it was the Hopi presence in northern Arizona that attracted the Mormons and influenced much of the Southwestern colonization (Peterson 1971: 194). Roads and trails used by Mormon settlers were first pioneered by Latter-day Saint missionaries to Arizona, and the Hopi presence was always a lure to the Mormon proselytizing spirit.

Elsie Talashoma of Bacavi was an accomplished quiltmaker. Her quilts featured her original designs of appliquéd and embroidered Hopi images. For many years she entered her beautiful quilts in the Museum of Northern Arizona's Hopi Craftsman Show. This 1966 photograph shows one of her baby quilts decorated with kachina dolls and rattles. Courtesy of the Museum of Northern Arizona.

Hopi Textiles

Within a very short time after the establishment of government schools and mission churches, quiltmaking became a commonplace and well-loved activity in every Hopi village. Churches around the country sent barrels filled with clothing, fabric, and quilts to be distributed among the Hopis. The donated quilts were not only practical, they were beautiful to look at with their colorful patchwork and appliquéd patterns. They offered additional inspiration to the novice Hopi quilters who were just learning the craft of piecing. Additionally, worn out quilts and blankets were also used as batting or filler for tied quilts. Hopi quilters soon developed a habit of utilizing every scrap of fabric that came their way, whether it was secondhand clothing, fabric scraps from sewing, or sugar and flour sacks. One quilter even recalled that her mother stitched a quilt from the small flannel sacks that held loose tobacco. The bags of

Hopi Craftsman Show, Museum of Northern Arizona, 1976. The *Koshari*, or Clown, Quilt was created by Elsie Talashoma. The images of the clowns are embroidered in black and rust colored threads. Courtesy of the Museum of Northern Arizona.

Hopi Baby Quilt by Bessie Humetewa, c. 1953, 40" x 40". Bessie Humetewa appliquéd and embroidered this original baby quilt top nearly fifty years ago. She decorated each block with the first toys that children are given at the Bean Dance, *Powamu*, in February, and the Home Dance, *Niman*, in July. The quilt blocks are stitched on linen squares, 9" x 9", with light blue sashing strips of line piqué. The blocks feature kachina dolls, rattles, a basket and a plaque, and a bow and arrow. Eileen Randolph recently quilted the top. Quilt courtesy of Eileen Randolph. Photography by David Elliott.

"Its A Girl" Quilt by Debra Kukuma, 37" x by 42", 1997. Debra machine pieced her original quilt with 1,200 tiny rectangles measuring 1½" x ¾". It is tied with a single strand of white yarn. Her custom-made quilts are in great demand for Baby Naming Ceremonies. Photography by David Elliott.

Joanna Quotskuyva and her grandson, Christopher Noonkester, with the Pinwheel Quilt he received at his naming ceremony, 1996.

cigarette tobacco could be purchased at the trading posts, and many of them had interesting designs printed on them. After the tobacco was used, the side seams of the bags were unpicked, the bags washed, and then they were all stitched together into a charming quilt top.

Fabrics and textiles have always been highly valued in Hopi culture. Cloth also holds great value among other Native American peoples. A length of fabric was often a prize for races and games. Yardage featured prominently in Giveaways among the Plains Indians, and swatches of colorful cloth were often used in costumes for ceremonial dances and in decoration of horses and other ritual accouterments. On the Plains, pieces of cloth were tied to the Sun Dance lodges as offerings and prayer requests. For as long as the lodge was standing, the fabric banners would wave in the wind and carry the prayers until the material wore away (Pulford 1989: 8, 49).

In Hopi society, a gift of clothing or fabric was highly ritualized into complex patterns. Articles of clothing and blankets were given to individuals at certain times of their lives, such as at birth, initiation, and marriage. Anthropologist Elsie Clews Parsons noted that a length of bright calico fabric was given to the mother at a Hopi Baby Naming Ceremony as one of the many gifts exchanged in the ritual (Parsons 1921: 98). Responsibilities of the giver were part of an intricate network of clan relationships. Certain items of clothing were also indicators of membership in societies or ceremonial groups. And when a person died, the clothing he was buried in would indicate his social and ceremonial status to the inhabitants of the Underworld (Wright 1979: 11).

At birth, a Hopi male received a small blanket woven of black and white cotton or wool fibers. Later, the child would be given a boy's kilt,

Baby Quilt, maker unknown, 41" x 37", 1996. The maker of this delightful baby quilt painted kachinas and rattles on the quilt blocks. The quilt is tied with pink embroidery floss. Photography by David Elliott.

The Hopi Snake Dance performed in late summer at Walpi attracted people from all over the country. Ex-President Theodore Roosevelt, hosted by George Babbitt, one of the Babbitt brothers of Flagstaff, Arizona, was hunting in the Buckskin Mountains north of the Colorado River during the summer of 1913. He wished to view the Hopi ceremony, so Babbitt took the group, which included two of Roosevelt's sons and Arizona Governor George W. P. Hunt, to the Hopi country. The large man, left center, wearing a cap and holding a hat in his right hand is Governor Hunt. His left hand rests against the right arm of Theodore Roosevelt. Roosevelt, like many other visitors to the Hopi mesas, was captivated by the Hopi people, their homes, and their ceremonies. After leaving Arizona he wrote several magazine articles describing his visit. Photograph courtesy of Dorothy O. Busath.

and eventually a kachina kilt at the time he was initiated, and other ritual garments as he began to participate in ceremonies. Girls also were given special clothing. A baby girl received a small blanket usually woven by her father or grandfather. As she grew she would be presented with a small version of the traditional woman's dress, and additional garments after her kachina initiation (Wright 1979: 12-15).

For her wedding, a woman receives traditional marriage robes, the *ova*, a belt, and wedding moccasins. Sometimes she also is given a dress, a blue blanket, and a special reed suitcase. These items are made by the male members of her groom's family. This costume is traditionally worn at *Niman*, the Kachina Going Home Ceremony, and in earlier times at the Baby Naming Ceremonies when her children are blessed. The wedding robe will be worn by a woman for the last time as a burial shroud, and "upon it she will travel to the Underworld" (Wright 1979: 20). In the hereafter she will become a cloud and bring rain for her people.

With the existing regard for cotton textiles, the introduction of sewing and quilting to Hopi women added another layer of appreciation for textiles in Hopi culture. As transportation and roads improved there was more opportunity to purchase fabric in trading posts and nearby towns, and women began sewing western style clothing for themselves and their families. In 1913 Theodore Roosevelt, one of the many tourists attracted to the Hopi country over the years, visited the mesas and wrote a description of the Hopi homes. He noted that he saw treadle sewing machines in several of the houses (James 1994: 171).

The Baby Naming Ceremony

Quilting activities among Hopi women spread with the introduction of sewing machines and garment production. Within a few short decades after the turn of the century, quilts were being made not only for warmth, but also for family and ceremonial objects. By the early 1920s, quilts were being used in Baby Naming ceremonies. Anthropologist Elsie Clews Parsons described a 1921 naming ceremony in which the paternal clanswomen gave quilts to the newborn (Parsons 1921: 58). In earlier times, a blanket woven by the child's father or a male relative was ritually

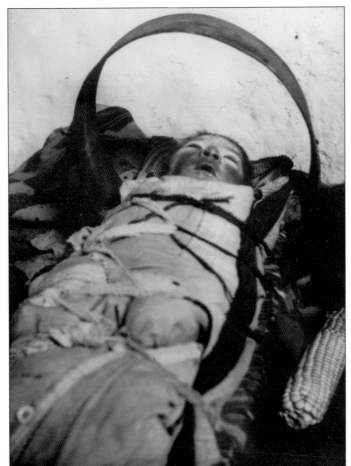

A newborn baby in a cradleboard lies on a pile of pieced quilts, c. 1905–1912. Next to the infant is an ear of the sacred corn. Courtesy of the Kate Cory Collection, Museum of Northern Arizona.

81

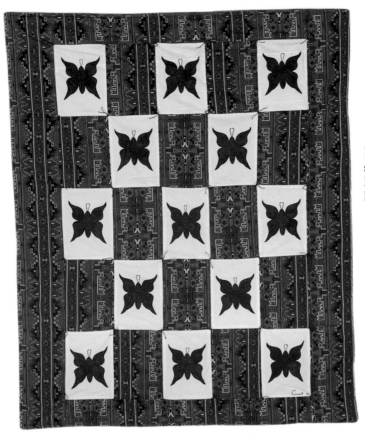

Butterfly Quilt, 1996. Painted and stitched by Lawrence Wester, Kykotsmovi. Photography by David Elliott.

Sun Forehead Quilt, maker unknown, 40" x 41", 1996. According to old Hopi stories, each clan got its name and identity from a sign or an incident that happened many years ago when the various groups of people were migrating to the Hopi country. It is said that one group arrived at Second Mesa just as the sun was rising, or showing its forehead. Those people became the Forehead Clan.

The maker of the Sun Quilt painted designs on white squares and added borders of geometric material in red, brown, and rust tones. The quilt is tied with light brown thread. Photography by David Elliott.

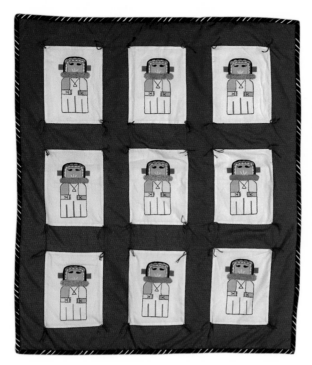

Kachina Quilt by Imogene Tewa, 45" x 38", 1997. Imogene Tewa lives in Moencopi. She paints kachina figures on her baby quilts and then ties them. These bright and appealing quilts are always in great demand for Baby Naming Ceremonies. Photography by David Elliott.

given to a newborn, but older Hopis relate that as quilting became more prevalent, baby quilts replaced the traditional woven blanket given at the naming ceremony.

Many Hopis believe that this tender ceremony, which welcomes a new life into family, clan, and tribal membership is one of the most meaningful and important rituals that they perform. Traditionally, when a child was born, the mother and baby were secluded in their home for twenty days. The door and windows of the house were covered so no bright light could shine in, and the child would not be exposed to sunlight until he was twenty days old. Even though most babies are now born in a hospital, it is still common for a bedroom at home to be prepared for the new mother and her child, and for some degree of seclusion to be practiced.

Kachinas and Rattles Quilt, 43" x 37", 1996, maker unknown. Kachina heads and gourd rattles have been hand painted on this colorful baby quilt. Photography by David Elliott.

A Hopi mother holding her baby in a cradleboard, c. 1905–1912. The baby is wrapped in a patchwork quilt. Courtesy of the Kate Cory Collection, Museum of Northern Arizona.

At harvest time or well before the birth of the baby, two perfect ears of white corn are selected and set aside. Corn holds deep symbolism for the Hopis, and with its special association with motherhood it is not surprising that corn plays an important role in this ritual. The perfect "mother" ears are placed next to the baby in the cradle, and will stay near the infant until the naming ceremony takes place. Later, they will be saved as a spiritual memento of the child's birth.

The paternal grandmother comes to the new mother's home early every morning to care for the mother and child. With sacred cornmeal she draws four lines on the walls of the room where the mother and baby stay. This symbolically creates a house for the baby. Every fifth day she will ritually wash the mother's and baby's hair in a special yucca soap. The new mother observes a ritual fast for twenty days. She will not eat

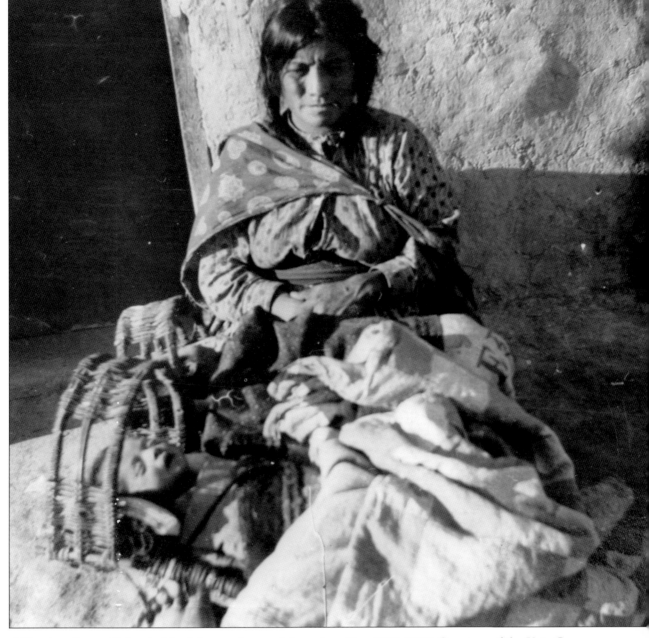

A Hopi mother with her babies lying under a patchwork quilt, c. 1905–1912. Courtesy of the Kate Cory Collection, Museum of Northern Arizona. (See detail page 89.)

meat, animal fat, or salt. Special foods will be cooked for her during this time. One traditional dish of whole cobs of corn cooked in water mixed with cedar leaves is always available to be offered to close friends and family who come to visit.

During the twenty days when the mother and baby are in seclusion there are many preparations for the naming ceremony. In earlier times the infant's father would make a cradleboard for the new baby. This is also the time when the aunts and family friends would make their baby quilts

Mesa Windows, 58" x 42", blue and gray corduroy quilt by Margaret Pacheco, Second Mesa, 1997.

and help with making *piiki*, a wafer thin ceremonial bread made with blue cornmeal, and other special foods for the naming ceremony.

The Baby Naming Ceremony takes place before dawn on the twentieth day. The infant's paternal grandmother and female relatives gather for a ritual washing and blessing of the baby. Each woman brings a small jar of water, which is used to wash the mother's hair. Then the baby is bathed in clean water. The child's head is gently washed by the female relatives who sometimes use the ear of corn as a brush dipped in the water and yucca root suds.

After the baby is washed, his face and sometimes his body is rubbed with white cornmeal. The grandmother then sits with the baby on her lap and wraps the child with a quilt that she has purchased or stitched for her new grandchild. After she wraps the baby with the quilt, she strokes the

Mudhead (*Koyemsi*) Quilt, maker unknown, 41" x 38", 1996. The *Koyemsi* appear at most dances. Sometimes they are drummers, they also announce dances, and they sometimes just entertain the people who have gathered to watch the dances. The mudhead figures on this quilt are hand painted on blocks of white flannel. The quiltmaker set the blocks with sashing panels of turquoise and a blue, gray, and dark turquoise geometric fabric. The quilt is tied with white embroidery floss. Photography by David Elliott.

child's breast with the mother ears of corn and says a blessing. She offers a prayer for the child to live a long life blessed with strength and good health. With her prayers she also offers a clan-associated name for the child.

After the grandmother has offered her prayer, other relatives and friends are invited to present their offerings. As each guest gives her blessing and a clan name, the baby is wrapped with another quilt. In earlier times, when blankets were all handwoven, a baby generally received only one covering, but today, with the great popularity of quilting, it is not uncommon for a baby to be given eight or ten clan names—along with an equal number of quilts—depending on how many relatives and friends choose to participate in the naming ritual.

Proud mothers today often describe the quantity of quilts that their child received in a naming ceremony, and relate that sometimes the baby and grandmother are nearly hidden under a mountain of gift quilts. Because quilts are in such demand for the namings, there is a ready market for baby quilts for any quilter who wishes to sell her work. Most people in a village know which quilter has quilts available, but it is not uncommon to see notes tacked on community bulletin boards advertising baby quilts for sale.

After the blessings and the gift of the names and the quilts, and just before the sun begins to show, the grandmother and mother take the baby, some cornmeal, and the two ears of corn and walk east toward the mesa edge and the rising sun. Here the baby is presented to *Taawa*, the Father Sun, and prayers are said to ensure that the child will grow in good health under his watchful presence. Anthropologist Edward T. Hall recorded that the prayers recited at this time were also for long life, and hopes that one would "grow old and bent until one's forehead touches the ground so that one can go into the next life" (Hall 1994: 72).

A Hopi boy carries his blanket across the plaza at Hotevilla, 1923. Courtesy of C. Burton Cosgrove.

A Hopi grandmother, holding the sacred ears of corn, gives a baby his first Hopi name, c. 1890s. H. R. Voth, photographer. Courtesy of the Arizona State Museum, University of Arizona.

Some of the cornmeal may be sprinkled toward the sun, and, in addition to the prayers that are said, the mother and grandmother repeat all of the special names that the child has been given. One early account of a Baby Naming Ceremony also stated that when the baby was taken outside to greet the morning sun, he was wrapped in all of the quilts that had been presented in the naming ritual (Beaglehole and Beaglehole 1935: 36).

After the final blessing, the mother, grandmother, and baby return home for a ritual feast of special foods. For this meal the father's family butchers a sheep, which is then cubed and cooked in a stew with hominy. The mother's family contributes baked breads, great quantities of *piiki*, and *pik'ami*, a traditional corn pudding. This pudding is an essential part of the feast. It is made of white cornmeal ground to a fine powder. Sprouted wheat that has been dried and ground is stirred in with a

A Baby Naming Ceremony, c. 1890s. An unidentified white woman is blessing the infant with the sacred ear of corn. At her right is the baby's mother and paternal grandmother. This blessing, which asks for a long and healthy life for the infant, is traditionally done at sunrise. Courtesy of the Mennonite Library and Archives, Bethel College, North Newton, Kansas, H. R. Voth photo.

greasewood stirring stick. Then sugar and boiling water are added. The pudding is poured into a large metal container and put into an underground oven where it is left overnight to bake. Huge quantities of *pik'ami* are made to feed the anticipated crowd of friends, family, and other villagers.

After the blessings, a crier stands on a rooftop and announces that everyone in the village is welcome to come to the home and eat. The oldest male in the house takes a small bit of food outside to be offered to the spiritual leaders and ancestors. More prayers are given asking for guidance in the life of the infant, and for the eventual blessing of more children for the family. Before the meal begins, the baby is fed. A pinch of corn pudding is dipped into the hominy stew and then placed in the child's mouth, and the grandmother tells the baby, "This is the food that we eat," and the other family and guests are then served. When the paternal relatives have eaten and are ready to leave, the mother and maternal relatives present them with gifts of *piiki* and pastries, a sort of ritual payment for giving a name. Any other leftover foods are given to the paternal grandmother.

Names are very important among the Hopi people, since a name gives an identity. Hopi belief does not distinguish between the temporal and the spiritual world. The name given to a Hopi enters him or her into an already established pattern, the clan system brings one into that life, and prepares the individual to be known as a Hopi when he goes into the

Painted Pottery Quilt by Bonnie Chapella, 65" x 47", 1996. Bonnie has set her blocks with patchwork sashing. Her quilt is a creative blend of Hopi design and traditional patchwork. Photography by David Elliott.

Joanna Quotskuyva and Barbara O'Bagy show one of Joanna's painted Hopi quilt tops, 1995.

next world. Names given at the naming ceremony always have a clan association, and the child will generally become known by one of the names that was offered.

At other times in a Hopi's life other names may be given, and they are all very important to the identity of the individual. The Baby Naming Ceremony honors a new life and weaves the child into a complicated network of family and clan relationships. But on a larger scale, the ceremony also reaffirms the membership and responsibilities of each individual within the Hopi community. With its emphasis on family relationships, the blessings and the ceremonial meal—made from the life-giving corn—the Baby Naming Ceremony is endowed with parallels that mirror the larger role of the individual within Hopi culture.

It is of no small consequence that the gift of a quilt is an integral part of the naming ritual. A gift of a quilt is a literal gift of warmth, as well as a tangible object endowed with the affection and good wishes of its maker or giver. It is a symbolic blessing. Long after the naming ceremony is over, a quilt endures as a palpable expression of love, and a link to the extended family members who will always be a part of the child's life. The quilts given in this important ceremony wrap each child within the circle of an ancient and tightly integrated community.

This 1959 photograph shows Remalda Lomayestewa and Martha Laban of Shungopavi. As Ms. Laban works on one of her coiled plaques, a folded patchwork quilt cushions her seat on the floor. Courtesy of the Museum of Northern Arizona.

Detail of a block from a baby quilt stitched by Elsie Talashoma for the 1969 Hopi Craftsman Show. The image of the "Mother Kachina" is hand embroidered. Courtesy of the Museum of Northern Arizona.

Quilts in Hopi Life

Quilts today are used in all aspects of Hopi life. They are used as blankets and bed coverings, ground cloths, window or door coverings, and couch throws. Within the family and clan network they are gifts of affection and esteem. Quilts also are wedding and birthday gifts. Grandmothers make quilts for their grandchildren, mothers make quilts for their sons and daughters who go away to school or to work in the cities. In addition to providing shelter, these quilts wrap the recipient in warm memories of home and family.

Hopi children grow up surrounded by quilts. They receive an amazing quantity of beautiful and colorful quilts at the naming ceremony, and they are given other quilts as they grow. Small children often incorporate quilts and quilt blocks into their play. A husband and wife anthropologist couple noted in the early 1930s that when children played "house" with their kachina dolls or the bone dolls that represent a "play family," they wrapped their dolls in pieces of baby quilt blocks (Beaglehole and Beaglehole 1935: 43). Hopi girls today are often given tiny quilts for their dolls.

The Hopi quilts that are commonly seen today are often the traditional patterns, including Log Cabin, Pinwheel, Spools, Irish Chain, and

Nine Patch. What makes many of these quilts unique, however, is the remarkable blending of traditional quilt patterns with Hopi images. One contemporary Third Mesa quilter pieced an Irish Chain Quilt, and then hand quilted a Hopi field of corn in the solid center blocks. The same quilter, Marlene Sekaquaptewa, also stitched a traditional Album Quilt with solid blocks alternating with the pieced blocks. In the solid blocks she quilted a spider and a web. The quilt is to be a gift for a family member who belongs to the Spider Clan.

Other quilters paint or appliqué Hopi designs on their quilts. One charming baby quilt was pieced in 1953 by Bessie Humetewa. The appliquéd and embroidered blocks depict the first toys given to Hopi children by the kachinas at the Bean Dance in February and the July Home Dance. The quilt features dolls, bows and arrows, rattles, a basket, and a plaque. Many contemporary quilters paint designs on their blocks with an oil-based fabric paint. The colors, available in a wide variety of hues, are permanent and the resulting blocks and designs are very striking. Some popular motifs are the Hopi rain clouds and lightning, kachinas, mudheads, clowns (koshari), baskets, and geometric basket and pottery designs.

Clan symbols also are found on quilts. Many clan names are related to animals and natural objects, and these images are readily transferred to surface design. Some clan-related motifs on quilts are corn, bears, snakes, eagles, and the sun. The butterfly is also a popular image; it signifies beauty and rebirth, and has been a common Hopi symbol for centuries. There is a Butterfly Clan and a Butterfly Dance, and the design appears on prehistoric Hopi pottery and in other ancient artifacts. Many Hopi quilters appliqué and piece butterfly quilt blocks, and one First Mesa woman, Karen Tootsie, created a remarkable Butterfly Kachina Quilt. She also has designed quilts depicting butterflies with the wings decorated with traditional Hopi pottery designs. Clearly, Hopi quilters have adapted traditional quiltmaking to their own unique culture and ceremonies.

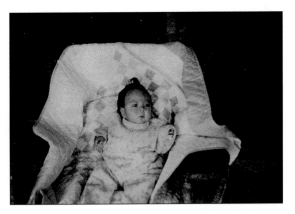

Mary Martha Baumgartner and her pieced baby quilt. Mary was born prematurely to a Hopi mother in 1940. Unfortunately, her mother and twin sister died in childbirth, and her family was unable to care for her. She was adopted by Mennonite missionary Maria Schirmer who had previously taken in three other Hopi children to raise. Photograph courtesy of Mary Martha Baumgartner.

Nine Patch Quilt by Rita Nuvangyaoma, 1997, Second Mesa. Rita hand pieced her bright Nine Patch Quilt with colorful yellow, pink, and orange fabrics. The blocks are set together with horizontal sashing strips and the quilt is tied.

Hand quilting is done less often than it may have been in the past. Hopi homes are not large and there is little room to have a quilt frame stretched out in the main living areas, although some women do baste their quilts together and quilt them in a small lap hoop. Tying is the more common method of finishing quilts. To finish a quilt in this way, the quilt top, batting, and lining are stretched out on a large table or basted into quilting frames. The quiltmaker then ties knots at intervals with yarn or string through all three layers of the quilt.

To tie quilts or have a quilting bee, women generally gather at a nearby church or at one of the village community centers. In the large public rooms there is space to put a quilt on the frame, and the quilters enjoy the socializing and talk that is always a part of the hours of working together. In the course of a morning spent sitting together at the quilting frame, news is exchanged, plans are made, and friendships are threaded together. As Karen Tootsie, a quilter from Keams Canyon stated, "We sew each other into our quilts. All the gossip, all the talk, and the sharing—it is all stitched into our quilts."

Imogene Tewa and her daughter Dannae. Imogene is a Moencopi artist whose hand painted baby quilts are always in demand for Baby Naming Ceremonies. Imogene also paints beautiful Hopi designs on rattles. The small rattles are popular gifts for babies or as Christmas tree ornaments.

The Quilt in Native America

Although it seems to be largely unknown to the public, quilting plays a prominent role in the daily and ceremonial life of many Native American groups. As with the Hopis, quilting was introduced to many Native Americans during the 1800s by missionaries and government schools. By the early years of the twentieth century quilting was becoming a common pastime on many reservations. Mrs. H. H. Clouse, wife of the Baptist pastor to the Kiowa Church at Rainy Mountain, Oklahoma, reported that for the year 1900–1901 the native women in her sewing group had made 72 quilts. Seven years later she recorded 230 quilts and garments made by Kiowa women (*Thirty-Six Years Among Indians* 1914: 30-32).

Miss Ida M. Schofield was a missionary at the Comanche Baptist Mission near Ft. Sill, Oklahoma. In 1900 she noted that several native women sewed quilts that were then sold, with the proceeds going toward a fund to help establish mission churches on other reservations (*Thirty-Six Years Among Indians* 1914: 39). Several years later Miss Schofield worked among the San Carlos Apaches in Arizona. She visited the camps every day and taught the Apache women to make quilts from the small

Hopis at Flagstaff, Arizona, 1901. There is little additional information with this vintage photo from the Bovee family collection, but the three Hopis are posed with a pieced quilt stitched with a popular all-over fan quilting design. Photo by Burton R. Bovee. Negative No. 52630. Courtesy of the Arizona Historical Society.

patches she gave them. After they learned to do piecework "instead of gambling they would sew patch work blocks" (*Thirty-Six Years Among Indians* 1914: 54).

In Florida, Seminole women who lived in the Everglades began stitching a distinctive patchwork style when hand-turned sewing machines became available to them (Williams 1992: 41). They create their own fabrics by machine stitching narrow strips of material together and then cutting crosswise across the strips. These pieced strips are then reassembled into remarkable geometric patterns. This bright, patchwork fabric is used mostly for clothing, and it is generally left unquilted.

Sandra J. Metzler-Smith documented the introduction of quilting to the Pomo culture in the North Coast Range in California, and stated that "by the 1870s, patchwork quilts were commonly made by the Pomo Indians of Mendocino County" (Metzler-Smith 1980: 45). The Pomo women were well known for their fine basketry, and Metzler-Smith indicated that many of the skills that went into coiling a basket were closely related to the work in piecing a quilt. "A good basketweaver made a good quiltmaker."

Like many native quilters, the Pomo women did not have easy access to fine fabrics and patterns for their quilts. They pieced quilt tops from secondhand clothing, mostly in geometrics and squares stitched from out-dated women's dresses and old men's woolen suits. Satins and silks, when they could get them, were especially treasured. The lack of quilt

Abandoned section of Oraibi on Third Mesa, 1923. Courtesy of C. Burton Cosgrove.

patterns was not a hindrance. Pomo women had been making baskets for centuries without using written directions, they saw the patterns in their minds. One Pomo quiltmaker even stated that if you used a book you would lose the patterns in your head (Metzler-Smith 1980: 45).

Across the United States, quilts soon became a common fixture in Honoring Ceremonies and Giveaways, ceremonies that celebrate births, marriages, graduations, and homecomings. Sometimes a Giveaway marks the end of a period of mourning. Quilts, cloth, money, and food are some of the gifts given in memory of the deceased, or as an expression of joy and thanks for other occasions. It is not uncommon for a family to distribute as many as twenty or thirty Star Quilts at a Giveaway. Quilts also are commonly seen at powwows where Native American groups gather for dances and Honoring Ceremonies. At the opening parades cars, trucks, and vans are often draped with quilts (Roberts 1992: 42).

Among the Plains tribes the Star Quilt is the most popular design and, generally, the most highly valued. In early times the star adorned clothing, shields, tepees, and buffalo robes. With the extinction of the bison herds—and the arrival of missionaries and the sewing bees—the Star Quilt replaced the buffalo robe (Martin 1988: 7). In addition to the use of quilts in ceremonial rituals, quilts are often seen in less solemn settings. One native village in Montana holds an annual Star basketball game for their high school team where Star Quilts are given to players, coaches, and officials for various achievements. A Dakota high school

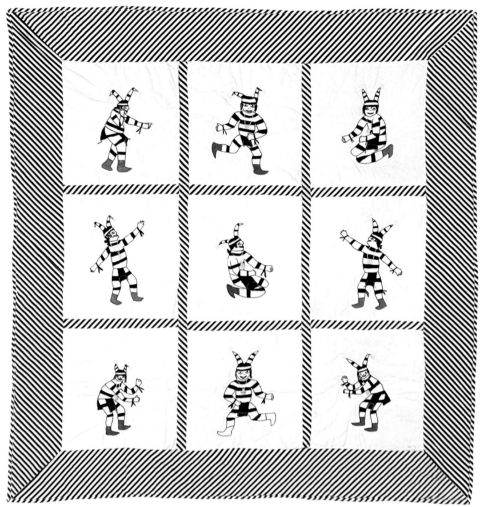

Hopi *Koshari* Quilt by Elsie Talashoma, 57" x 55", 1975. The *Koshari* appear at spring and summer dances. Their bodies are painted in stripes of white, from kaolin, and black, from soot or corn smut. The black circles around their eyes and mouths have lines that extend out to the temple and ear. They wear striped, horned headdresses made of sheepskin with cornhusk tassles at the tips, and rattles made of animal hooves tied about their knees or ankles. The clowns function as entertainment for the audience at dances and ceremonies, however, their sometimes outrageous actions are also social commentary or sanctions against improper behavior (Wright 1994: 78).

The delightful images for the Hopi Clown Quilt were designed and embroidered by Elsie Talashoma. The clowns are wearing medicine bags, breechcloths with red and green tassels, and rust-colored boots. Their horned hats have yellow tassels. Elsie machine quilted around each figure and each block. The blue and white sashing fabric is cut on the bias, and the imaginative use of striped material set at an angle to the quilt blocks adds to the excitement and movement of the clowns. Quilt courtesy of Bruce and Marlene McGee. Photography by David Elliott.

Nine Patch Quilt by Rita Nuvangyaoma, 1997, Second Mesa. Rita hand pieced and quilted her Nine Patch Quilt. She prefers hand sewing over using the sewing machine. The patchwork blocks are set with alternating solid pink blocks.

celebrates a Star graduation where instead of caps and gowns, the graduates wrap themselves in a Star Quilt for the walk up to the podium to receive their degrees.

Quilts also find a special use in funerals. Among most Anglo groups, quilts are only used or shown at a funeral if there is a special significance to a quilt or quiltmaking for the deceased or one of the family members. In earlier times, funeral quilts were often made from pieces of the deceased person's clothing, and in rural areas quilts were often used as burial shrouds or to line a homemade coffin. Today, although a quilter often finds great solace in stitching a quilt in memory of the deceased, it is uncommon to see a quilt used in a funeral service. One exception is a popular line of quilts that are specially created as liners for a casket company (Gebel 1995: 210).

Quilt historian Carol Williams Gebel has documented the role of quilts in the final rite of passage. She noted early examples such as a quilted textile from a tomb of a Scythian chieftain dating from 100 B.C. to 200 A.D., and the use of quilts as burial shrouds during the time of the American Overland Trail experience (Gebel 1995: 207). Geographically, her documentation of the use of quilts as funeral objects ranged from Russia to the Polynesian Islands to Africa.

Gebel found extensive use of quilts in funerals among Native American tribes. Chickasaw women often made a quilt to lay out the deceased or to drape over a casket. The Sioux often wrap the body of the deceased in a Star Quilt before placing it in the coffin, and quilts are often the first things offered when a Giveaway is part of a funeral service (Gebel 1995: 212-17). For many Indian people the Star Quilt represents a continuing link between the living and the dead.

Because quilts are associated with warmth and comforting, Chickasaw quilters often stitched a quilt to keep the body "warm" until the burial. Additionally, a quilt often was laid over a coffin to muffle the sound of dirt as the grave was filled. The Oklahoma quilt documentation project discovered two examples of Chickasaw quilts that were made when a child was born, and were then saved to be used for his last rites (Oklahoma Quilt Heritage Project 1990: 24, 88).

Among the Hopi people, quilts are also commonly used during the last rites of passage. One reason for the use of quilts in a burial is that the Hopi mesas are some distance from a town and funeral homes. Distances and transportation difficulties often make it impractical to seek out an urban mortuary. More important, however, is the traditional practice among the Hopi of having the closest male relatives prepare and bury the deceased, generally within a few hours of the death. If a person's soul is ultimately to become a kachina and help to bring rain and blessings to the Hopi people, burial and its accompanying rituals must all be completed by sundown of the fourth day after death.

With all of the visual pleasure and warmth that quilts inherently embody, and because burials are conducted by the closest family members, it is only logical that quilts are commonly used as burial shrouds among the Hopi people. The Hopis do not have a tradition of using caskets for burials, since wood is much too scarce, and the practice of laying out the body for public mourning and viewing is not a part of Hopi tradition. But the deceased is dressed in certain articles of ceremonial clothing, and a quilt is most often used as the final wrap. Babies who die are wrapped in their small quilts, sons and daughters are wrapped in the quilts pieced by their mothers, aunts, and grandmothers, and quilters are often covered by a special quilt that they had stitched together.

From birth until death, quilts hold a special place in Hopi life. Quilts have important utilitarian roles. Quilting is a social as well as a creative outlet for the many Hopi women and men who are active quilters, and quilts signify special ritual functions in Hopi ceremonial life. Quiltmaking may have been an introduced art form, but over the last century quilts have become tightly interwoven into Hopi life. Hopi quilters have blended traditional patterns and techniques with their own cultural designs. They have integrated the quilt into their ancient society, and, in the process, they have created their own rich and meaningful quilting heritage.

Helen Sekaquaptewa at her ranch house, *Paagwuvi*, south of Kykotsmovi, October 1980. One of Helen's patchwork quilt tops used as a couch cover is visible against the back wall of the living room. Courtesy of the Arizona State Museum, University of Arizona, Helga Teiwes, photographer.

The Quilters

Many Hopi quilters participated in the Hopi quilt project and exhibit at the Museum of Northern Arizona. Some were intensively involved in helping with the plans, others made a quilt for the exhibit. Some contributed stories and histories, while others chose not to be as deeply committed, and some requested, partly because of cultural considerations, that their names not be used. A heartfelt debt of gratitude is extended to all of the quilters, no matter what their level of participation. Without their interest and enthusiasm this project would never have become a reality. Many thanks.

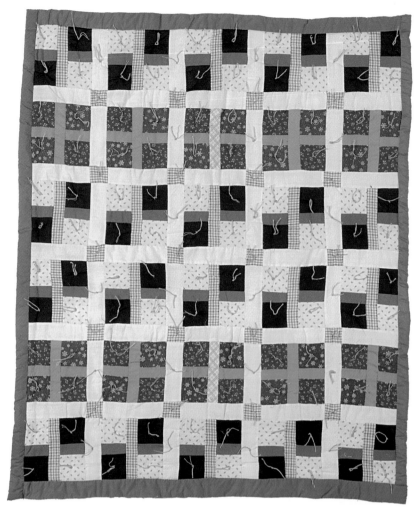

Four Patch Variation by Helen Sekaquaptewa, 51" x 41", 1988. Helen hand pieced this Four Patch Quilt when she was ninety years old. She used muslin for the sashing and a red and white plaid for the setting squares. The quilt is tied with a light turquoise-colored string. Quilt courtesy of Allison Lewis. Photography by David Elliott.

HELEN SEKAQUAPTEWA

Helen Sekaquaptewa was born in 1898 in Old Oraibi. She was known by her Hopi name of *Tuwawisnima*, "trail marked by sand." In her village at that time, two factions were developing. The Friendlies were those who welcomed some of the changes brought by the white people. They sent their children to the day school built below the mesa. The Hostiles were more conservative and traditional. They resented both the intrusion of whites into their land and the government agents sent out from Washington. Helen's parents were among the Hostile group, and they resisted sending their children to the government school. Each morning truant officers and Navajo policemen came up to the village to search for children who were not attending school.

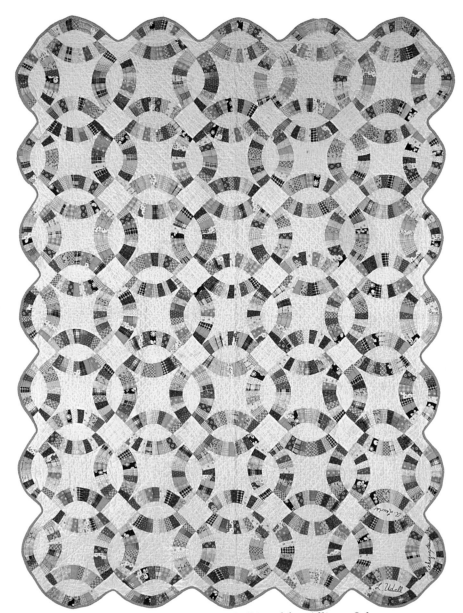

Wedding Ring Quilt, 88" x 64", 1969. Pieced by Allison Sekaquaptewa Lewis. Quilted and signed by Allison Lewis, Helen Sekaquaptewa, and Louise Udall. Photography by David Elliott.

In her autobiography, *Me and Mine*, told with her friend, Louise Udall, Helen related how her parents would hide her from the policemen each morning. One hiding spot was in the *piiki* storage cupboard hollowed out from a wall. Another place was in the rabbit blankets that were hung from the ceiling beams by their four corners. Eventually, she was caught and sent to school where she was given an Anglo name, Helen.

In September 1906, the Hostiles were driven out of Oraibi by the Friendlies. All they were allowed to take with them were the food and

"First Hostile Camp." When the Hostile group was forced to leave Oraibi in 1906, they walked a few miles to the west. A temporary camp was set up using blankets and quilts strung among the trees for shelter. One of the refugees was Helen Sekaquaptewa who recalled that the weather turned cold and it began to rain. As the frigid water dripped down on the people huddled under the trees, the dyes from the blankets ran, and the colors from the fabrics streaked the people's faces with red, green, and blue. Courtesy of the Museum of Northern Arizona.

blankets that they could carry. The people walked a few miles to the west where they stopped and built shelters of brush, quilts, and old blankets. A few vintage photographs exist of this refugee camp, and the patchwork patterns of the quilts can plainly be seen as they were strung among the juniper trees. A few days later the weather turned cold and rainy. Helen later told her children that the dyes in the quilts and blankets were not colorfast, and as the water dripped down upon the people huddled below, their faces became streaked with the red, yellow, and blue colors from the blankets.

Eventually the people built a new village, but still they were not allowed to follow their traditional ways. One morning just a few weeks after they fled Oraibi, they awoke to find their camp surrounded by troops who had come to take the children away to school at Keams Canyon, thirty-six miles to the east. Helen's father and several of the men from the Hostile faction were sent away to prison at Fort Huachuca in southern Arizona. Helen was not allowed to go home until the following year when school ended. She was then eight years old.

In the four years that Helen was at Keams Canyon, her mother was able to visit her only twice. With the arrival of a new superintendent in

1910, the children were not allowed to go home at all during the summers. Helen worked in the school laundry, and later, when she attended the Phoenix Indian School, she worked in the sewing room. The Home Economics Department had a large production room where all of the uniforms for the students were made. Here Helen learned clothing construction, and her work was always so fine that she was employed by teachers and nearby families to do sewing for them. Helen worked for Dr. Brown, the school's superintendent, for many of the years that she was in Phoenix.

Helen married Emory Sekaquaptewa in 1919. They lived in Hotevilla on Third Mesa and raised ten children. Naturally, Helen sewed for her large family, and she recalled how pleased she was when Emory purchased her first sewing machine in 1934. It was a Singer treadle machine, one of the first in the community. Helen continued to sew for others in order to earn extra money. Several of the government employees always hired Helen to stitch their uniforms (Sekaquaptewa and Udall 1989: 191).

According to her daughters, quilting was always Helen's first love, and she made many quilts over her lifetime. In the early years she pieced her quilts by hand, but later she used her Singer to stitch her quilt tops. One of her aunts who lived in Phoenix often sent old clothes. Whatever couldn't be used by Helen's family was cut into quilt pieces. Using heavy weights of fabric she made "clumsy quilts," pieced floor mats to sit on at traditional meals.

Hopi cornfields at Moencopi, 1938. Photograph courtesy of the Utah State Historical Society. All rights reserved. Used by permission.

Helen never bought a quilt pattern, all of her piecing and quilting designs were hand drawn. She also hand quilted most of her quilts, and taught those skills to her daughters, Allison and Marlene. One pattern that she commonly used was the all-over fan design drawn lightly with pencil. Knots were tied in a string at intervals, and by holding the end of the string at a center point and progressively moving the pencil out to each knot, she could draw successive arcs across the top of her quilt.

Helen's quilting frames were lengths of 1" by 3" boards held at each corner with clamps. Strips of denim from old jeans were tacked onto the wood frames, and the quilt top was fastened to the fabric. Helen ripped apart castoff woolen clothing from the mission church boxes, cut it into squares, and sewed them all together to make an even batting for her quilts.

For a time, Helen made her own cotton batts. One of her relatives was married to a Pima man who worked on one of the big cotton farms in the southern part of the state. There he gleaned cotton from the fields and sent it up to Helen packed into bags. Helen cleaned and carded the cotton, but it was hard and tedious work. She eventually decided to go back to the batts she made from old clothing.

Helen's children remember that she was very creative, and how she could just "put things together" and they always came out looking beautiful. Some of her favorite patterns were the Bow Tie, Fan, Nine Patch, and Log Cabin. She also made a few appliqué quilts and a number of whole cloth quilts. These quilts have no piecing or appliqué on the top, but they are covered with beautiful hand stitched designs. Her sewing and quilting was so beautiful that one daughter recalled that on washdays Helen "lost" many garments and some quilts while they were hung out to dry.

Helen met Louise Udall when she moved her children to Phoenix during the winters so they could attend high school. Louise was the mother of six children. Two of her sons later became very well known for their government service. Morris Udall was a member of the House of Representatives for Arizona, and Stewart was Secretary of the Interior under Presidents Kennedy and Johnson. Louise was also a Mormon, and each week she would go out the nearby Maricopa Reservation to attend the Relief Society quilting bees. Helen had been quilting for years, and she enjoyed the company of the Maricopa women at the weekly bees. She also sang with the Singing Mothers group. The two women quickly became close friends and Louise often spent summers up at Third Mesa with Helen and her family.

Helen was eventually baptized into the Mormon church, and she especially enjoyed the quilting projects with the Relief Society ladies. She wrote that quilting was a year-round activity. "We pieced tops from this and that and got out linings here and there. For our filling, there was wool from the sheep that we could wash and card, or we could buy a cotton batt from the Sears Roebuck catalog, if we had the money" (Sekaquaptewa and Udall 1989: 244).

Hopi Field of Corn, 98" x 74", 1997, by Marlene Sekaquaptewa, Bacavi. Marlene stitched corn plants into the solid center blocks of her traditional Irish Chain Quilt because corn is the essence of Hopi, both economically and spiritually—it is food, it is ceremony, "our whole life is based on the corn." As Marlene pieced her top she thought about putting corn on the blocks because she wanted it to look like a field of corn. She chose the fabrics to reflect the colors of the cornfield, "the colors around us," the earth tones and the soft colors of the sun on the landscape. Marlene's son helped her draw the quilting pattern for the corn. It took a lot of work to get it right. It is only on cardboard now, but she will put it in plastic to save it. It is a pattern she would like to use again in another quilt.

When Marlene's brother, Emory, saw the quilt he said that it reminded him of children. The Hopi word for the new ears of corn is the same word used for children, *tiimat*. Marlene believes there are parallels between tangible things. The Hopis believe that the way you take care of your plants is the same way you take care of your children. They both have to be reared and cared for. The fruits of that effort is beautiful corn—enough to eat. And the parallel is healthy children to perpetuate your society. Life goes on.

Helen and Louise remained close friends for two decades. In 1974, Louise was diagnosed with cancer. She was trying to finish one last quilt for her son. The top was pieced, but she did not think that she would be able to finish the quilting in time. Helen learned of the quilt that Louise was trying to complete, so she helped to organize a quilting. Louise was too ill to sit at a quilting frame, but Helen put the quilt on the frame and then Louise's friends began to arrive. Louise lay on a couch and visited with the quilters. Many of the Maricopa women came by to quilt, along with other friends and neighbors. Helen stayed at the house until the last stitches were taken in the quilt. She brought a sheepskin rug that she placed on the floor under the quilt. When she grew tired from sitting at the quilting frame, she just rested on the rug, near Louise, and in the middle of all of the quilting activity (see Appendix).

The quilt was finished within a few days, and Louise lived to see it presented to her son. Soon after, she passed away and Helen spoke at her funeral. She recalled the good times they had shared shelling corn, harvesting, singing, and especially, quilting.

Helen lived to the fine age of ninety-three, and she made quilts almost until her last days. She always wanted to stay busy, and piecing and quilting was the one activity that helped her stay productive and creative. Helen passed away in 1991. She left behind many quilts and unfinished tops—and a legacy of love and caring that can be felt in each of her stitched creations.

ALLISON LEWIS AND MARLENE SEKAQUAPTEWA

Helen's love of quilting is shared today by her daughters, Allison Lewis and Marlene Sekaquaptewa. They both do fine piecing and hand quilting, and they both know how to draw original quilting designs on their many quilt tops. Marlene recalled that there was always a quilt in some stage of progress in her mother's house. There were tops that she was piecing or one in a quilting frame. When Helen taught her daughters to quilt she always spoke of putting quality and skill into their work. She said, "Make a good quilt, take the smallest stitch possible, and it will last a long time."

When Helen's children were grown and began to have their own families, she always planned special quilts for her grandchildren. Sometimes she would admire one of her pieced tops that was being made for a grandchild—and then she would often decide to add more blocks and borders to make it larger, so the child would be able to enjoy it longer than if it were just a baby quilt. Most of these quilts were hand quilted because Helen would rather quilt than tie a top. She considered hand quilting an art form that also made the quilt more durable, and when a quilt was covered with fine quilting it reflected her pride in creating a beautiful piece of handwork.

Helen said that when you give a quilt to a child, part of you goes with that quilt, and it creates a special tie with that child. Today Helen's daughters continue to practice her fine quilting tradition. They are both beautiful quilters who share their talents with their families.

Allison had three boys, and she sewed all of their clothes: t-shirts, jumpsuits, and pajamas. Her quilts were pieced from the scraps left from her sewing. Allison especially enjoyed the times when her mother came to stay with her. Then they quilted together, and while they quilted, Helen sang Hopi songs. Those were special times.

Allison remarked that she enjoyed planning a quilt, and watching the pattern develop—even though she never felt that she was as good as her mother at seeing it in her mind. The Wedding Ring Quilt is really sentimental to Allison. She pieced it in 1969, and everything in it came from the things she had sewn for her family. In March of that year her father went into the hospital. He was dying. Allison put her quilt on the frame, and over the next eight weeks, between visits to the hospital, Allison, Helen, and Louise Udall worked on the quilt. It was finished that spring, and Emory died on May 15. Each of the women wrote their names on the quilt, and Allison embroidered over the writing with black thread. The Wedding Ring Quilt holds many memories.

Marlene also sewed for her family of five children, but now that her family is grown she has more time for quilting. She has made quilts for all of her grandchildren and many nieces and nephews. Marlene is very interested in preserving her Hopi heritage, and many of her quilts blend traditional patchwork with hand quilted imagery that reflects some aspect of Hopi life. Her Irish Chain Quilt is quilted with a field of Hopi corn. A traditional Album Quilt has alternating blocks stitched with spider webs, a gift for a family member who was born into the Spider Clan.

Marlene is also interested in the strong textile heritage of her people. She has been experimenting with traditional Hopi dyes and various

Visitors to Walpi watch a Snake Dance in 1918. On the left is George Kennedy, a trader at Chinle, Arizona, Miss Lucy Jobin, Emry Kopta, a sculptor and artist who lived among the Hopi for many years, and Miss Buckman. Perhaps the quilt in the lower center of the photo was used by Hopis or visitors to sit on while watching the ceremony. Photograph courtesy of J. W. Kennedy.

cottons, and is planning to stitch a landscape quilt with those special fabrics. Marlene now spends most of her time at her mother's home in Kykotsmovi, and every morning when the light is best in the south room, she spends a few hours quilting. And when a quilt is finished, she stitches on a binding using a decorative blanket or feather stitch. That is the way her mother taught her to finish a quilt.

ALTA SEYESNEMA

Alta Seyesnema was a basket maker from Shipaulovi on Second Mesa who always had a special talent for making beautiful things with her hands. She probably learned to quilt from her mother, who went to the quilting bees held on Saturdays at the Sunlight Mission, the church built just below the mesa. Alta did much of her sewing by hand, although her mother owned a treadle sewing machine. One daughter said that she always felt safer using that treadle machine when it was raining; you never knew what might happen with all of that thunder and lightning when you were using an "electric."

Alta loved handwork, she could sew clothing, crochet, knit, quilt, and tat with her silver tatting shuttle, as well as make the beautiful baskets for which Second Mesa women are so well-known. Alta made quilts from scraps, flour sacks, and even mattress ticking. She had some Anglo friends who frequently sent her boxes of cloth for her quilting or

Janice Dennis with her Long Hair Kachina Quilt, 54" x 42", 1997, Kykotsmovi.

to stitch up into clothing for her family. She often sewed the White Cross blocks together into strips for her quilts. She pieced aprons, and even made some from discarded neckties.

Alta had a talent for making quilting patterns. She could look at a quilt, and then sit down and draw her own patchwork templates. One daughter recalled watching her draw a diamond. She worked on the pattern, getting the size and the angles just right. And then she proceeded to make a quilt from her hand-drawn pattern. She always sewed by hand, and she was very fast. She would take several small running stitches and then pull the thread through all of the stitches at once.

Referring to her creative abilities, one daughter simply said, "My mother was a fancy lady." Alta passed on her talents to her children, and her four surviving daughters are all well-known basket makers and quilters. Tatting was the only craft that the daughters did not learn from their mother. Today Pearl Nuvangyaoma, Rita Nuvangyaoma, Mary Jane Batala, and Frieda Yoyhoeoma can all weave magnificent baskets and plaques, and stitch beautiful quilts—and their daughters are also following in their artistic legacy.

Margaret Pacheco holding two of her corduroy quilt tops, 1997, Second Mesa.

Rita Nuvangyaoma with her Log Cabin Quilt, 69" x 56", 1996, Shipaulovi. Rita hand quilted this bright Log Cabin Quilt pieced with red and blue fabrics.

PEARL NUVANGYAOMA

Pearl Nuvangyaoma is a prolific quiltmaker, and sewing is one of her most enjoyable pastimes. She remembers that as a girl of five or six, she would go with her mother to the Sunlight Mission to sew. Pearl says that she has always made quilts. Some of her quilts are stitched from traditional patterns such as the Pinwheel, Nine Patch, and Trip Around the World. However, sometimes she doesn't feel like following a rigid pattern, and then she just enjoys putting the colors and textures of many pieces of cloth together. Those original quilts are a delight to the eye and radiate a sense of spontaneity and captivating graphics.

DEBRA KUKUMA AND MARGARET PACHECO

Debra Kukuma and Margaret Pacheco are Pearl Nuvangyaoma's daughters, and Alta Seyesnema's granddaughters. Margaret remembers playing with her great-grandmother's old treadle sewing machine. She did sew on it a few times, but mostly she recalls sitting on the foot treadle below the machine and rocking back and forth. Following in their family tradition, Margaret and Debra are both well-known basket makers and beautiful stitchers.

Debra makes quilts from tiny squares and rectangles arranged into marvelous geometric patterns. Most of her quilts are stitched from corduroy, and the tiny blocks are laid down with the grain of the fabric set at right angles to each other—"crosswise"—so the pieces don't slip. All of her pieces are stitched together by hand.

Debra also cuts all of the pieces by hand, and they are carefully stacked into piles arranged by colors. She says she has to be organized to plan out her quilts. Then she lays the small squares and rectangles out on her bed to make an interesting pattern. When she was asked the approximate number of tiny pieces she uses in each quilt, Debra replied, "I just put them together, I don't count them!"

The beautiful graphics in Margaret Pacheco's quilts are the result of her artistic eye, rather than through her sister, Debra's, method of careful cutting and planning. Margaret simply cuts the corduroy fabric by eye and lays the pieces down, starting with the smaller center pieces, and building her quilt out to the size she wants. Then, explaining that she is too impatient to sew by hand, she just "runs it through the machine." Margaret's favorite part of the process is in piecing her wonderful, original tops. Then she often folds them up and goes on to the next one. She says she always has a stack of tops that she will finish "someday."

When asked where they got all of the corduroy for their quilts, Margaret and Debra explained that they go up to the community center at Shipaulovi and go through the boxes of secondhand clothing that are donated to the village. They pull out all of the corduroy pants and cut them in half, and "she takes one leg, and I take the other."

Both Debra and Margaret have busy lives with families and children to care for. During the daytime, they work on their baskets, but in the evenings after supper, they get out their boxes of fabric and work on piecing their imaginative and beautiful quilt tops.

NAMPEYO AND BONNIE NAMPEYO SAHMIE CHAPELLA

Nampeyo, one of Hopi's most famous potters, was credited with the revival of Hopi pottery in the late 1800s. She was born in 1860 in the village of Hano on First Mesa, a village founded nearly two hundred years earlier by a group of Tewa people who had migrated from the Rio Grande Valley in New Mexico to the Hopi country. Nampeyo's father was a Hopi, Quootsva, of the Snake Clan, from Walpi and her mother, White Corn, of the Corn Clan, was Tewa.

Nampeyo learned to make pottery from her mother, but it was not until she visited the Hopi ruins of Sikyatki at the edge of First Mesa, and saw the intricate patterns on the ancient pottery shards there, that she began to paint the beautiful designs for which she later became so famous. Those Sikyatki shards provided her early inspiration, but it was her own artistic genius that enabled her to create the graceful pottery that

Nampeyo, c. 1920. C. M. Wood, photographer. Courtesy of the Arizona State Museum, University of Arizona.

Bonnie Chapella with one of her original quilts, 1996, Keams Canyon. Each block is hand painted with Hopi pottery designs, and the blocks are set with patchwork sashing. Bonnie is a potter and a fifth-generation quiltmaker.

she painted with precise and original stylized designs representing eagles, bats, birds, butterflies, and other motifs. During her lifetime Nampeyo's pottery was widely collected and appreciated, and today her priceless pottery is displayed in museums and art galleries.

It is a little known fact that Nampeyo was also a quilter. Her granddaughter, Daisy Hooee, recalled that when her grandmother's Anglo friends brought her fabric, she often stitched it into quilts for her family to use. Daisy stated that Nampeyo said, "I'm going to make a blanket, a quilt…I have a big family and I have to give them blankets" (Kramer 1996: 96).

Although none still exist, Nampeyo's quilts were probably not made with traditional quilting patterns. Most likely, they were just serviceable comforters, stitched together from scraps of fabric and worn out clothing, such as wool and denim. But Nampeyo's daughters were quiltmakers—just as they also shared her legendary skills for making beautiful pottery—and one great-granddaughter still has a rare quilt top stitched together by her great-grandmother, one of Nampeyo's daughters. For the Nampeyo family, as with most Hopi women, quilting was simply a practical and necessary activity. They made quilts to keep their families warm during the frigid months of a northern Arizona winter. Their quilts were made of pieces cut from castoff clothing, or from the quilt blocks that they could get from the missionaries at the Baptist church in Polacca. Fabric was valued, every scrap was thriftily used.

Karen Tootsie with her hand painted Butterfly Kachina quilt top, 1997, Keams Canyon. Karen added Seminole pieced borders to the painted blocks for her Butterfly Kachina Quilt.

Edison and Karen Tootsie, 1997, Keams Canyon. Edison's mother taught him to crochet when he was a boy, and he still finds it a relaxing and creative activity, along with piecing quilt tops. Edison crocheted this queen-size bedspread several years ago, and now it serves as a bright coverlet.

Bonnie Chapella is a great-great-granddaughter of Nampeyo. She is also a fifth-generation quilter. Her great-grandmother, Annie Healing, did patchwork, her grandmother, Rachel Namingha, made quilts at the Polacca Baptist Church, and her mother, Priscilla Namingha, also stitched quilts for her large family. Most of the women of the Nampeyo family learned to quilt at the Baptist Church where there were sewing classes for girls on Saturdays. The lessons started with embroidery and crochet, and then they stitched aprons and hemmed scarves. Eventually, they worked up to patchwork, piecing quilt tops by hand from the donated quilt blocks because there were few sewing machines in the Hopi villages during the first decades of the twentieth century.

Bonnie is the youngest of eight children. Her mother pieced quilts out of old clothing, fabric scraps, and flour sacks. When she had nice patches she made Star Quilts and another pattern called the Shadowbox. This block has a center square of one piece of fabric surrounded on all four sides by framing strips of a second fabric, often of a darker hue. This creates a two-dimensional, or shadowbox, effect.

Bonnie blends the family tradition of making exquisite pottery and beautiful quilts. Bonnie's quilts are unique because she paints traditional family pottery designs on her quilt blocks. The blocks are then pieced into quilt tops with original strip-pieced borders. The white fabrics for her hand painted blocks often come from the 25-pound sacks of Blue Bird Flour sold at the nearby trading post in Keams Canyon. Her favorite colors are the rust and brown earth tones. Her quilts are beautifully planned and stitched into striking geometric designs. They are pieces of art—a sophisticated blending of quilting skills and traditional Hopi design.

EDISON AND KAREN TOOTSIE

Edison and Karen Tootsie live in a beautiful spot on the eastern edge of the Hopi Reservation near Keams Canyon. High sandstone walls rise above their home, and each day the brilliance of the rising and setting sun washes the canyon in a golden glow of light. Edison and Karen are both proficient needleworkers. As a boy, Edison went to the Baptist Church with his father for the men's sewing and quilting meetings. He related that his grandfather sewed grass mats for window coverings. His grandfather would gather long grasses that grew wild near their home and lay them flat. Then he would stitch along the edges and across the middle to make a square or rectangular mat of a size that would fit into a window.

Edison does not knit, as many Hopi men of an earlier generation did, but his mother taught him to crochet, an activity that he finds a relaxing pastime. He learned to sew from watching his father at the men's church gatherings, and today he enjoys designing and piecing quilt tops. Two years ago he gave each of his children one of his handmade quilts for Christmas.

Karen learned to sew by watching her grandmother, but she states that she never enjoyed the sewing in Home Economics classes as a girl. Her grandfather could also sew and knit. He would knit leggings with colored bands at the top and bottom, and he would knit cables and other designs into the long stockings that are sometimes used in Hopi ceremonies. When he retired he enjoyed knitting as he watched his favorite television programs, the daytime soap operas. Because he could knit without watching his hands, he never missed a scene on the television screen.

As an adult, Karen became interested in quilting, and taught herself how to make quilts by reading pattern and design books. All of her early quilts were just tied, but now she also does a lot of hand quilting. Several years ago, as part of her church outreach, she began holding quilting bees for the elderly ladies, donating her time and whatever quilting supplies she could gather together. At first the meetings were held in people's homes, but the groups grew larger as more women heard of them, and they began to meet at the community centers. Karen holds quilting bees with the elderly at Polacca, at Shipaulovi on Second Mesa, and she also works with the Navajos at White Cone.

In addition to piecing quilts, Karen also has a wonderful talent for painting. Many of her quilts are pieced with blocks that have been painted with designs of children's toys and juvenile storybook characters, butterflies, flowers, and Hopi boys and girls. Karen Tootsie is a multitalented, generous, and giving quiltmaker. Her willingness to teach and share her quilting skills embodies the best qualities of the American quilting spirit and tradition.

In Orchard at Ranch 1962.

Louise Udall and Helen Sekaquaptewa, 1962. In the orchard at the Sekaquaptewa ranch. Photograph courtesy of Elma Udall.

Appendix

"The Quilting" was written by Eloise Udall Whiting shortly after her mother, Louise Udall, passed away in 1974. Louise pieced this special quilt for her son, Stewart Udall, Secretary of the Interior, from the many satin and velvet robes he had been given by various universities when he received honorary degrees. This simple tale of a group of Anglo and Native American women coming together to finish a quilt reveals much about the enduring bonds between women, and of the friendship and caring expressed through a seemingly unremarkable activity such as gathering together for one last time around a quilting frame.

THE QUILTING

January 16-19, 1974

Wasn't that a quilting?

She was going to die soon. We knew and she knew but none of us spoke of it directly. When I got there ("Get the hell out there," Burr had said), she had turned yellow or more of a bronze orange. She was having Elma [another daughter] add her signature to her checking account and signing over the car to Elma, but none of us spoke too directly.

And there lay the pieced velvet quilt top... bright reds and rich purples and deep blues in square and rectangular shapes. Stewart had received more than twenty honorary doctorates in law and liberal arts over the years and had been given the hoods from each—velvet hoods with satin or grosgrain linings, things of beauty especially to someone who loved cloth as she did. Robert Frost had a king-sized quilt made of his, and that was a good idea. She had been wanting to get to this project for several years but had not picked up the hoods from Stewart's until last summer. The operation in the early fall had got in the way of really hurrying the quilt; but, as she recuperated, she cut the hoods and began piecing. When she saw there weren't enough pieces, she had supplemented the velvets with some of her rag shop brushed knits—Harvard and Rag Shop side by side, we said.

When I was there for two weeks to visit in November and had inquired of her what projects we would do, thinking of cleaning closets and woodwork, she had said we would piece the quilt because to her a project meant only one thing... sewing. Her Turley granddaughters helped piece too. (Inez had noted that as Mom was waiting for Christopher to drive her to Tucson in September, she had said, "I had a lot of things I still wanted to do; but if this is the end, I've had a good life.") The quilt probably was at the top of the list of "a lot of things I still wanted to do."

Baby quilt made by Elsie Talashoma of Bacavi. This quilt was entered in the 1969 Hopi Craftsman Show at the Museum of Northern Arizona. The center blocks of the quilt are hand appliquéd and embroidered. The center portion of the quilt is hand quilted with a tied outer border. Courtesy of the Museum of Northern Arizona.

And there lay the pieced velvet quilt top. And there she lay on the couch with not enough energy to get the quilt finished. She had planned to go to Aunt Edna's after Christmas when Elma would leave for Washington and she was alone. (ALONE AT LAST! she had written when we had all left after seeing her one by one in October and November.) Aunt Edna lived 200 miles away and had a quilting room with the frames always up. They would spend a week and quilt adding the batting and the lavender brushed knit backing—just two excellent quilters quilting around each piece. I had said on the phone before I came, "Let's do the quilt while I am there," and Elma chimed in, "We could all drive to Aunt Edna's for a few day's visit," but she hadn't said anything. Elma and I are lousy quilters and weren't in her plans.

The beautiful Sun Quilt was featured in the 1965 Hopi Craftsman Show. Unfortunately, the maker of the quilt, as well as its whereabouts today, is unknown. However, this magnificent quilt features fine pieced and appliqué work. The background is quilted in a fan design, and the sun image is outline quilted with radiating lines stitched from the sun face out to the triangle edging. Courtesy of the Museum of Northern Arizona.

And there lay the pieced velvet quilt top. I got in on Monday. Tuesday Elma and I whispered to each other that the trip was out and maybe a quilting in the dining room would be our next best bet—the sooner the better so that she could be a part of it. You quilted and you visited at the same time. But we'd talk it around so it would be her idea. Also, now that Helen [Sekaquaptewa] had come to spend some days after an urgent message, we could count on Helen to quilt beautifully. Wednesday we went shopping for the quilt batting, Mom, Elma, Helen, Jessie (visiting for the day from Flagstaff), and I, and Mom was too weak she almost couldn't walk from one store to another. We knew even more surely the Wellton trip was out.

Elma called Gaius Tuesday and asked without a definite date, "Could you get us some quilting frames if we decide to quilt?" We had not yet talked to Mom about having a quilting soon. How do you word it? So there it was Wednesday afternoon and there was Howard at the door with quilting frames, beside himself with pleasure at being able to do something for his favorite ex-neighbor. I called, "Here comes Howard with some quilting frames," and Mom, drowsing on the couch exhausted from the shopping venture, sat bolt upright and said, "Damn!"

For an hour we worked at getting the frames just right—which chairs to set them on and how to put the clamps. Howard kept a running commentary going on how he used to help his mother tie quilts by sitting underneath the quilt and pushing the needle and yarn back up to his mother. I saw him squeeze Mom's hand once. She stood in the background a bit and gave some advice, but left it to Helen to show us how to spread the top or thumb tack. The quilt was tacked, and we had a quilting on our unprofessional hands.

Elma said to Mom that if we had gone to Aunt Edna's, Mom might have one good day and two bad ones while we were there but Mom didn't answer.

A phone call to Marlinda Graham, the Relief Society President of the disbanded Lamanite Ward, and a phone call to Bernice to please let Aunt Edna know was about all the direct contacts we made about the need for quilters. Helen, who could coax some Indian tea or gruel down Mom's unsettled stomach (mom ate piki and even a whole piece of Allison's fry bread when she gave up on white men's food), began quilting before bedtime.

Joanna Quotskuyva's painted Hopi quilt.

122

Hopi Girl Quilt by Milfred Dallas, Jr., 46" x 46", 1997. Milfred is a talented designer and quiltmaker from Hotevilla on Third Mesa. He has many original patterns for his painted quilt blocks, but some of the most popular are the quilts he makes for Baby Naming Ceremonies. Milfred decorates the custom-made baby quilts with the clan emblems of the mother and father of the new baby. He also sews pillows and aprons, and creates spectacular cakes and centerpieces for weddings and other special events.

Karrie Yoyhoeoma, Shipaulovi, 1996. Karrie Yoyhoeoma is a fourth-generation quilter from Second Mesa. She often sews with her mother and aunts. Her favorite quilts are color-coordinated and planned, rather than the scrap quilts made by many quilters.

Thursday saw five Indian faces (Helen Sekaquaptewa, Allison Lewis, Marlinda Graham, Florine Coops, Maxine Moore) around the quilt with Mom sitting with them some and quilting a little but lying down more. Stella Downey of Ninth Ward, who is one of Mom's quilting friends, happened by and was pleasured to quilt. Alice Overson, now living in Mesa, came over to visit and quilted. Gail Turley taught to quilt by Nana years ago, also quilted in the evening and spent the night with us as she was a substitute—teaching locally. Helen would rest on the floor under the quilt when she was tired, admiring her stitches, we said. Allison furnished tamales and beans and other delights. By Thursday night we had begun to roll the quilt a turn or two.

Friday found some new and some repeat Lamanite faces, and we laughed that the Lamanite stitches outnumbered the Anglo and they were all stitches of love and friendship. When anyone happened by and admired the quilt (two men installing the new stove—too late, Elma said—or the county photographer taking a picture of Mom for a dinner in her honor), there was always talk of buying it. Mom said to anyone who would listen, "This is the girls' idea." She sadly declared that her stitches didn't look right and that she couldn't hold the needle. When it was over and Helen was taking out some of the bigger stitches, Mom said gloomily, "I bet they're mine."

There was a knock on the door Friday evening and there without notice stood Aunt Edna brought by her granddaughter. All she said to us was, "Will you let me in?" She didn't say much to Mom nor Mom to her, but did she quilt! Helen had left for the reservation with Allison, being gone from Mom's house from Friday afternoon until Monday; so there sat Aunt Edna alone pushing that needle in and out. I tried a stitch or two but got laughed at. Elma never picked up a needle.

Saturday afternoon Elda Brown and her daughter showed up. Aunt Elda knew there was a quilting, but thought she would visit an hour and go on to see her great granddaughter. Four hours later after a quilting marathon by two determined quilters, the last stitches were done and we took off the quilt. Aunt Elda represented those good old St. Johns days beautifully. Aunt Edna immediately began binding the quilt, still not visiting (tears were too near), although she did take time out to play some of the old tunes on the piano.

Sunday was a day of rest with Aunt Edna leaving early and crying hard outside away from Mom. Inez and I even went to church and Burr and Alice came over for his birthday complete with Mary Coyle ice cream brought by them. The next day Mom rode with them to the airport which was her last time away from the house.

Monday Helen and Allison walked in, much amazed that the quilt was done. Mom wanted a finer binding, and Allison helped her mother cut out strips. Gaius came that day all set to quilt her share and was rather startled to see the quilting frames banished. Undaunted, she inspected the underside of the quilt (bona fide quilters look at the back to see the pattern the stitches make and admire their smallness rather than the prettier front), gleefully finding three places that had been missed. Furnished with needle and thread, she sewed the places and afterward took the frames home.

Several days later, Elma said to Mom, "Have you forgiven us yet for quilting without your permission?" with not much of a reply. But I finally heard Mom say in puzzlement, "But I didn't know anyone would come to quilt..."

And there lay the finished pieced velvet quilt...

Yes, wasn't that a quilting?

Bibliography

Abbott, Sarah E.
1900 *Annual Reports of the Department of the Interior, Indian Affairs.* Washington: Government Printing Office.

Adams, David Wallace
1995 *Education for Extinction: American Indians and the Boarding School Experience, 1875–1928.* Lawrence: University Press of Kansas.

Baker, J. C.
1889 *Annual Reports of the Department of the Interior, Indian Affairs.* Washington: Government Printing Office.

Beaglehole, Ernest, and Pearl Beaglehole
1935 "Hopi of the Second Mesa." *Memoirs of the American Anthropological Association* 44.

Boyer, Diane, and Susan Lowell
1989 "Trading Post Honeymoon: The 1895 Diary of Emma Walmisley Sykes." *Journal of Arizona History* 30 (4): 417–444.

Brooks, Juanita
1944 "Indian Relations on the Mormon Frontier." *Utah Historical Quarterly* 12 (1–2): 1–48.

Christensen, C. L.
1922 "Among the Hopis." *The Times Independent*, March 9, 1922, Moab, Utah.

Collins, Ralph P.
1892 *Annual Reports of the Department of the Interior, Indian Affairs.* Washington: Government Printing Office.

Flake, David Kay
1965 *A History of Mormon Missionary Work with the Hopi, Navaho and Zuni Indians.* Unpublished Thesis, Brigham Young University.

Frey, J. B.
1915 *A Review of the Rise and Progress of the Mission Activities of the General Conference of Mennonites of North America.* North Newton, Kansas: Board of Foreign Missions.

Gebel, Carol Williams
1995 "Final Rite of Passage Quilts." *Uncoverings.* San Francisco: American Quilt Study Group, Vol. 16, 199–227.

Hall, Edward T.
1994 *West of the Thirties: Discoveries Among the Navajo and Hopi.* New York: Doubleday.

James, Harry C.
1994 *Pages from Hopi History.* Tucson: The University of Arizona Press.

Johnson, Abigail
1933 *Beyond the Black Buttes: True Stories of Hopiland.* Kansas City: The Western Baptist Publishing Company.

Kent, Kate Peck
1983 *Prehistoric Textiles of the Southwest.* Albuquerque: University of New Mexico Press.

Kramer, Barbara
1996 *Nampeyo and Her Pottery.* Albuquerque: University of New Mexico Press.

Martin, Christopher, ed.
1988 *Native Needlework: Contemporary Indian Textiles from North Dakota.* Fargo: North Dakota Council on the Arts.

McClintock, James H.
1985 *Mormon Settlement in Arizona.* Tucson: The University of Arizona Press.

Means, Florence Crannell
1928 *Diary.* Collection of Eleanor Means Hull, Colorado Springs, Colorado.

1960 *Sunlight on the Hopi Mesas.* Philadelphia: Judson Press.

Metzler-Smith, Sandra J.
1980 "Quilts in Pomo Culture." *Uncoverings.* San Francisco: American Quilt Study Group, Vol. 1, 41–47.

Quilting bee at the Oraibi Mennonite Church, 1893. The Hopi women preferred to sit on the ground to do their piecing. Courtesy of the Mennonite Library and Archives, Bethel College, North Newton, Kansas, H. R. Voth photo #92.

Moody, William A.
1959 *Years in the Sheaf: The Autobiography of William Alfred Moody.* Salt Lake City: Granite Publishing Company.

Oklahoma Quilt Heritage Project
1990 *Oklahoma Heritage Quilts: A Sampling of Quilts Made in or Brought to Oklahoma before 1940.* Paducah: American Quilter's Society.

Parsons, Elsie Clews
1921 "Hopi Mothers and Children." *Man* 57–58 (7): 98–104.

Peterson, Charles S.
1971 "The Hopis and the Mormons 1858–1873." *Utah Historical Quarterly* 39 (2): 179–194.

1973 *Take up Your Mission: Mormon Colonizing Along the Little Colorado River 1870–1900.* Tucson: The The University of Arizona Press.

Pulford, Florence
1989 *Morning Star Quilts.* Los Altos, California: Leone Publications.

Roberts, Chris
1992 *Powwow Country.* Helena, Montana: American & World Geographic Publishing.

Rules for Indian Schools.
1890 Annual Reports of the Department of the Interior, Indian Affairs. Washington: Government Printing Office.

Schirmer, Maria
1918 April letter to the Board of Foreign Missions, Mennonite General Conference. North Newton, Kansas: Missionary Correspondence Files, Mennonite Library and Archives, Bethel College.

Sekaquaptewa, Helen, and Louise Udall.
1989 *Me and Mine: The Life Story of Helen Sekaquaptewa.* Tucson: The University of Arizona Press.

Sells, Cato
1916 *Tentative Course of Study for United States Indian Schools.* Washington: Government Printing Office.

Southwest Indian Mission Records
Salt Lake City: L. D. S. Church Archives.

Suderman, Mabel
1938 January letter to Evalyn Bentley, Arizona Historical Society.
1938 April letter to Evalyn Bentley, Arizona Historical Society.

The Independent
1937 Halstead, Kansas, November 26.
1942 Halstead, Kansas, June 19.

Thirty-Six Years Among Indians
1914 Chicago: Woman's American Baptist Home Mission Society.

Truax, W. B.
1875 *Reports of the Commissioner of Indian Affairs.* Washington: Government Printing Office.

Voth, Martha Moser
1892 *Diary.* North Newton, Kansas: Mennonite Library and Archives, Bethel College.

1894 "From the Moqui Mission," *The Indian's Friend* 6 (6): 6.

Walker, William H.
1996 *Homol'ovi: A Cultural Crossroads.* Winslow: Arizona Archaeological Society, Homolovi Chapter.

Whiteley, Peter
1988 *Bacavi: Journey to Reed Springs.* Flagstaff: Northland Press.

Williams, Charlotte Allen
1992 *Florida Quilts.* Gainesville: The University Press of Florida.

Wright, Barton
1979 *Hopi Material Culture: Artifacts Gathered by H. R. Voth in the Fred Harvey Collection.* Flagstaff: Northland Press.

1994 *Hopi Kachinas: The Complete Guide to Collecting Kachina Dolls.* Flagstaff: Northland Publishing Company.

Young, Louise A.
1896 "Other Peeps into the Work." *The Indian's Friend* 8 (9): 8–9.

Additional titles available from Sanpete Publications…

Pioneer Quiltmaker

The Story of Dorinda Moody Slade, 1808–1895
By Carolyn O'Bagy Davis

Pioneer Quiltmaker is the story of a nineteenth-century woman who settled the untamed frontiers of Texas and Utah. Through her travels and tragedies, Dorinda pieced and stitched her original quilt patterns. Her exceptional skills and creativity are reflected in her stunning quilts that endure as a striking contrast to the sorrows and hardships of her pioneer life. *Pioneer Quiltmaker* features 43 color images, illustrations, and 33 vintage photographs. Foreword and patterns by Helen Young Frost.

Pioneer Quiltmaker – 8 ½" x 11", 80 pages, $17.95

A Quilt for the Promised Valley

By Carolyn O'Bagy Davis

A Quilt for the Promised Valley, a sequel to *Pioneer Quiltmaker*, is the story of the creation and travels of an extraordinary quilt created by Dorinda Slade. Through the decades since its creation in 1866, the Sunrise in the Pines Quilt has survived as a legacy of humble faith and a pioneer woman's remarkable artistic talent. In addition to both color and vintage photographs, this book contains Helen Young Frost's pattern for the Sunrise in the Pines Quilt.

A Quilt for the Promised Valley – 8 ½" x 11", 64 pages, $17.95

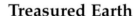

Quilted All Day

The Prairie Journals of Ida Chambers Melugin
By Carolyn O'Bagy Davis

Quilted All Day is the biography of a remarkable prairie woman, a sod house homesteader and quiltmaker who recorded her daily life in decades of journal entries. Ida's quilts and diaries are extraordinary pieces of women's history. *Quilted all Day* has 61 color images, and 39 vintage photographs. Foreword by Barbara Brackman. Patterns by Helen Young Frost.

Quilted All Day – 8 ½" x 11", 128 pages, $21.95

Treasured Earth

Hattie Cosgrove's Mimbres Archaeology in the American Southwest
By Carolyn O'Bagy Davis

Hattie Cosgrove was a hardware store heiress who came to the West in 1907. She was soon captivated by the Mimbres culture of southwestern New Mexico and the beautiful painted pottery found in the ruins. Her efforts to preserve and document Mimbres sites led to an esteemed career as an archaeologist with Harvard University. *Treasured Earth* contains a Foreword by Richard B. Woodbury, as well as illustrations, 210 vintage photographs, and over 400 of Hattie's Mimbres bowl drawings.

Treasured Earth – 8 ½" x 11", 204 pages, $24.95

Additional copies of **Hopi Quilting** may be ordered at $27.95.
Shipping: $3.95 for the first book, $1.50 for each additional book.

SANPETE PUBLICATIONS

P. O. Box 85216 • Tucson, Arizona 85754 • (520) 622-6007